ENGLISH LANGUAGE TEACHING in Theological Contexts

Kitty Barnhouse Purgason, editor

WILLIAM CAREY
LIBRARY

English Language Teaching in Theological Contexts
Copyright ©2010 by Kitty Barnhouse Purgason

Unless otherwise indicated all scripture quotations taken from the New American Standard Bible®, Copyright © 1960, 1962, 1963, 1968, 1971, 1972, 1973, 1975, 1977, 1995 by The Lockman Foundation. Used by permission.

Published by William Carey Library
1605 E. Elizabeth Street
Pasadena, CA 91104 | www.missionbooks.org

Melissa Hicks, copyeditor
Amanda Valloza, graphic design
Josie Leung, graphic design assistant
Felicia Hartono, graphic design intern
Rose Lee-Norman, indexer

William Carey Library is a ministry of the
U.S. Center for World Mission
Pasadena, CA | www.uscwm.org

Printed in the United States of America

14 13 12 11 10   5 4 3 2 1 BP1000

Library of Congress Cataloging-in-Publication Data

English language teaching in theological contexts / Kitty Barnhouse Purgason, editor.
    p. cm.
  Includes bibliographical references and index.
  ISBN 978-0-87808-464-7
  1. English language--Study and teaching--Foreign speakers. 2. Theology--Study and teaching. I. Purgason, Kitty Barnhouse.
  PE1128.A2.E496 2010
  428.2'4--dc22
                                    2010024539

Contents

Part A: Contexts and Programs

Part B: Materials

Introduction

Kitty Barnhouse Purgason
kitty.purgason@biola.edu

Kitty Purgason trains ESL/EFL teachers in the Department of Applied
Linguistics and TESOL at Biola University. She has a Ph.D. in
Applied Linguistics from UCLA. She grew up in India and has taught
in Korea, China, Turkey, and Turkmenistan.

A man from Myanmar anticipates theological studies in a Manila
seminary drawing students from all over Asia ... in English. A Korean
couple prepares for missionary service in Indonesia through an
international agency in which the lingua franca is ... English. A woman
from Japan studying in a seminary in Los Angeles writes her dissertation
... in English. A young man from Poland arrives in Michigan ready to
train for the priesthood and eventually do parish work in Montana ...
in English. Seminary students in Ukraine eagerly look for resource
materials, but find that they haven't been translated yet and they will
need to read them ... in English. These are the reasons for this volume
on English language teaching in theological contexts.

Some of these contexts are in the U.S., where most theological
institutions have non-native English speaking international students, either
preparing to study or needing language support while they are in school.
At some campuses, 20-40 percent of the student body is international. A
few U.S. schools have nearly 100 percent international students.

Theological institutions around the world also have English teaching
needs. In some contexts, English is the medium of instruction because of
the wide variety of languages spoken by students from around the region.
In others, English is needed because of the dearth of theological materials

in local languages—students need a strong reading knowledge of English in order to access theological resources. Thirdly, English may be taught to students who need it for future international work. This is especially true among the expanding missionary forces from Asia and Latin America.

These growing needs coincide with trends in the field of Teaching English to Speakers of Other Languages (TESOL) which have produced valuable models for the teaching of English in theological contexts.

English for specific purposes (ESP) has been a trend since the 1980s with growing numbers practicing and researching business English, medical English, English for the hospitality industry, and so on (e.g., Dudley-Evans & St. John 1998, Basturkmen 2006, Harding 2007). The time has come to acknowledge theological English as well, or English for Bible and Theology (EBT).

One of the tenents of ESP is that specialized areas of study have their own lexicon and discourse patterns. To read theological materials or to write papers in theology classes, students need to learn this specialized language. Work in ESP provides models for researchers developing materials for EBT.

Another hallmark of ESP is a focus on teaching specific skills that students need, rather than general language skills, in order to maximize the short time students have available for study before their professional duties. Learning specialized English may not only be more time-efficient, but also more motivating. Depending on where they are and why they are studying, theological English students may focus on:

Reading: the Bible; theological texts; journal articles; Bible reference materials such as dictionaries, commentaries, and concordances; and other materials such as Sunday School curriculum and mission agency handbooks.

Writing: papers; prayer letters; etc.

Speaking: prayer; testimony; Bible study; group discussion; preaching.

Listening: lectures; Bible studies.

Besides ESP, another trend in TESOL which researchers and practitioners have long been working on is English for academic purposes (EAP) (e.g., Jordan 1997, Flowerdew & Peacock 2001, Hyland 2006). Attention has been paid to such specifics as reading in law classes, engineering classes, and so on. The time has come to attend to those whose academic pursuit is theology.

A specific type of EAP which has been applied in some of these theological contexts is content-based English as a second language (CB-ESL) (e.g., Snow, Brinton, & Wesche 1989; Snow & Brinton 1997). In this model, students learn English while they are also learning academic content. It has proved to be both motivating and effective, both in the general academic world, as well as in seminary ESL programs.

Within the general purview of ESP is a branch focusing on English in the workplace (EWP) (e.g., Belfiore & Burnaby 1995). Typically concerned with jobs such as hotel housekeepers, mechanics, food service employees, workplace ESL teachers and materials developers are attuned to the specific language demands of their students' jobs. Their insights can also be applied to the demands of Christian workers, particularly missionaries who are not native speakers of English but who have specific tasks they need to accomplish in English during their work.

Thus, with ESP, EAP, CB-ESL, and EWP firmly established in the field of TESOL, there are good models available for those working in the areas of English for Bible and theology, both in study and work contexts.

This book began with a colloquium at the 2002 national convention for Teachers of English to Speakers of Other Languages, our professional association. Five practitioners of English language teaching in theological contexts in the U.S. spoke about the programs and materials they had developed. The audience was eager to hear more, especially from people working outside the U.S., so in 2003 the colloquium featured speakers working in seminaries and Christian schools in Brazil, Lithuania, India, the Philippines, and Korea. The needs are so many and so diverse that people wanted even more—that call was the seed for this book. I have tried to solicit contributions that represent the diversity of the theological English world: English for study as well as daily use; English for low-proficiency as well as advanced students; English for reading, writing, speaking, and listening (the traditional "four skills"); small struggling programs as well as well-funded programs associated with large institutions; programs serving both Catholic and Protestant seminaries and Bible colleges; and programs from Asia, Europe, and South America, as well as North America.

The first half of the book consists of descriptions of various theological contexts and English teaching programs. My goal is to describe both the language teaching challenges inherent in various places, and the solutions offered by various programs. Schwenke, Poleski, and Spencer describe very different ESL programs for international theology students in the U.S.— one is about a seminary which is part of a larger university with a large intensive English program, the other two are about smaller seminaries which developed their own ESL programs. Altena and Mawhorter are about schools of theology whose ESL programs focus on writing, a major concern for North American seminaries with non-native speakers. Chapters 6 through 12 feature theological schools in a variety of nations: India, Slovenia, Russia, Ukraine, Philippines, Brazil, and Korea. Adapting to change is a common theme in Devadason, Sesek, Ryan, and Thorpe. Whereas the goals of the programs in the earlier chapters are mostly academic, involving reading and writing, there are also English for theology programs with goals related to oral skills and with students who are not traditional seminarians, described in Alvarez, Dormer, and Truitt.

The second half of the book focuses on specific materials. It is my hope that these samples will inspire readers to develop their own materials following the models provided. Additionally, if the students for whom the materials were developed are similar, readers may be able to use the materials themselves. The first three chapters in this section describe fairly extensive materials covering reading, writing, speaking, and listening. Among them, Yee and Azariah exemplify two types of content-based materials, theme-based and adjunct; and Dormer describes communicative integrated skill materials. Theology-specific reading and listening materials are sorely needed—the topics of Ryan, Schoenfeld, Burke, and Thorpe. Whereas most of the materials covered in this section are unpublished materials, the chapters by Pierson are about published materials to help students with reading, grammar, and vocabulary. Vocabulary is also the topic of the final chapter by Lessard-Clouston.

For readers working in a school where students need to learn English and theology at the same time, I hope that this book will provide encouragement and information about the range of programs and materials which are currently being developed. For readers interested in new developments in English for specific purposes and content-based language instruction, I hope that the examples in this volume will add to the body of knowledge about these areas of TESOL.

References

Basturkmen, H. (2006). *Ideas and options in English for specific purposes.* New York: Routledge.

Belfiore, M. & B. Burnaby. (1995). *Teaching English in the workplace* (2nd ed.). Markham, Ontario: Pippin/OISE.

Brinton, D., Snow, M., & M. Wesche. (1989). *Content-based second language instruction.* Boston: Heinle.

Dudley-Evans, T. & M. St. John. (1998). *Developments in ESP.* Cambridge: Cambridge University Press.

Flowerdew, J. & M. Peacock (Eds.). (2001). *Research perspectives on English for academic purposes.* Cambridge: Cambridge University Press.

Harding, K. (2007). *English for specific purposes.* Oxford: Oxford University Press.

Hyland, K. (2006). *English for academic purposes.* New York: Routledge.

Jordan, R.R. (1997). *English for academic purposes.* Cambridge: Cambridge University Press.

Snow, M. & D. Brinton (Eds.). (1997). *The Content-based classroom.* New York: Longman.

Acronyms

CB-ESL	Content-based ESL
EAP	English for academic purposes
EBT	English for Bible and theology
EFL	English as a foreign language
ELT	English language teaching
ESL	English as a second language
ESP	English for specific purposes
EWP	English for the work place
iBT	Internet-based TOEFL
NNS	Non-native speaking
TEFL	Teaching English as a foreign language
TESL	Teaching English as a second language
TESOL	Teaching English to speakers of other languages
TOEFL	Test of English as a foreign language
TWE	Test of written English (used to be part of TOEFL)

Part A: Contexts and Programs

Chapter 1

Serving Seminary Students with a University Intensive English Program

Karen Schwenke
karen.schwenke@biola.edu

Karen Schwenke has been teaching ESL in the United States for more than twenty years. She is now an Assistant Professor and the Academic Coordinator for the English Language Studies Program at Biola University in La Mirada, California.

Talbot Theological Seminary is one of the seven schools of Biola University. Its place in a university with an overall enrollment of 5,700 students enables its non-native speaking (NNS) students to be served by an intensive English program, the English Language Studies Program (ELSP). Nearly 10 percent of the Talbot student body is on international student visas and about three quarters of those are from Korea, with the rest from various other nations. This chapter describes how ELSP prepares these Talbot students, while at the same time it serves students preparing for other graduate and undergraduate schools at the university.

ELSP offers classes at six levels, focused on skills such as listening, reading, grammar, speaking, and writing. It has a full-time director, a full-time academic coordinator/faculty member, two additional full-time faculty, four to six adjunct faculty (depending on enrollment), a number of teaching assistants, and two administrative assistants. Enrollment over the years has ranged from 120 to 150 students.

Clearly this is a rich resource to offer the NNS students of Talbot. However, there are also challenges. ELSP students range from college freshmen who are not sure of what they want to major in to mid-career pastors with advanced degrees in their home country seeking an American theological degree. This chapter will first describe the benefits, and then discuss the difficulties of such a program.

Benefits

One benefit to having an intensive English program is that Talbot is able to accept students who are a good fit for the seminary but whose English is not yet up to an adequate academic standard. International students who have not taken the TOEFL[1] or whose score is less than one hundred (internet-based TOEFL; paper TOEFL 600) are told by admissions that they will have to take the Biola English Placement Exam (BEPE) during their orientation a week before classes begin. Students accepted to Biola, but placed in the lowest ELSP classes based on their BEPE scores usually spend three semesters working on English before taking any seminary classes.[2] Students who are placed in the fourth of six levels (with a BEPE score that is roughly equivalent to a TOEFL score of seventy-nine internet or 550 paper) may take concurrent seminary classes during the three semesters that it takes them to move through levels four through six. Once they have completed the last level of ELSP, they continue to take general seminary writing classes, which include native speakers, during the following two semesters.

About 70-75 percent of the students in the ELSP are preparing for Talbot. Thus, another benefit to Biola's program is that along with English language skills, the curriculum can focus on the type of work and participation that is expected of students in graduate seminary classes. ELSP is able to offer students the support needed to make the transition between academic work in their home countries and the U.S. The goal is to prepare students to be better able to deal with the seminary material, participate in class, and graduate.

A key aspect of the support that is offered involves the curriculum. One example of the specialized materials that have been developed is a downloadable voice file of faculty pronouncing common theological

---

1   This includes students who cannot afford the TOEFL, who work in a place where it is not convenient to take it, or who have been too involved with ministry to study for this high-stakes exam.

2   Although this policy may be seen as helpful to students who otherwise would not be able to attend Talbot, some students end up being shocked at their placement and worried about the time and expense it will require for them to get up to the required standard in English to begin classes at Talbot.

vocabulary and other commonly mispronounced words. Another example is taped lectures from core Talbot classes for use in the second and third-level listening classes.[3] Students are required to sit in on actual seminary lectures and take notes for their third-level listening class in anticipation of the type of listening and class participation they will encounter the following semester when they may start taking seminary classes. In addition, with input from Talbot staff, students are taught how to communicate with professors and department staff as well as how to participate in seminary classrooms. Readings from Talbot textbooks and materials are used in classes in a variety of levels and classes. Finally, each level writing class is given a library workshop on the university standards for academic honesty and avoiding plagiarism.

Some extra-curricular resources are also available. Talbot students are recruited to lead a Bible study to help ELSP students become accustomed to the type of personal sharing that is required in an American seminary. They are also recruited as conversation partners to help ELSP students practice interaction.

Challenges

However, there are also challenges to serving a broad spectrum of students. One is that students come in with a wide range of both background and interest in theology. Within Talbot, there are students who are preparing for work in Christian education, theology, missions, pastoral work, and teaching. There are students who have already studied theology in Korea and are familiar with the content, if not the language. Other students, however, are called to the ministry, but may be novices in terms of theology. These differences are intensified when one considers the non-Talbot students served by ELSP who may be preparing for a graduate degree in multicultural education or an undergraduate degree in music or science. This means that a placement test which is meaningful and accessible to a seminarian (including, for example, a reading passage about Martin Luther), will be much more difficult for a freshman art major. In classes, students with less theological expertise often hesitate to participate if the content of the class material seems too theological, preferring instead to defer to their more theologically experienced classmates so that they are not embarrassed by their lack of knowledge. Therefore, it is important that ELSP instructors focus on language and academic skill learning and re-iterate throughout the semester that the content is simply a means to that

---

3   See Burke, chapter 18.

end. Likewise, instructors need to remind students that they will not be tested on their knowledge of the content, but rather on their ability to use the content to demonstrate their language and academic skills.

Another challenge is to develop an atmosphere of equality in classrooms with both graduate and undergraduate students who come from cultures with a high sense of hierarchy. The graduates tend to be older with some even being close in age to the parents of the undergraduates. At the beginning of the semester especially, instructors have to work hard to help the students understand the dynamic needed in a language classroom. Students are open to changing their behavior, but it can take time and practice. Even after direction from the instructor that everyone is equal and free to express ideas, there have been instances where undergraduates were taken aside by older Talbot Korean students and told not to participate until after the older students had talked and not to disagree with their elders.

A third challenge stems from the fact that many of the Talbot students have already been pastors and are used to being given a great deal of respect in everyday interaction. Now there is nothing in their appearance to distinguish them from other college students, and in terms of language they may be at the bottom of the heap. When instructors get to know them and show admiration for what they have accomplished, the students feel better about the daunting task in front of them. Feedback must also be given with humor and respect.

A final challenge is encouraging Korean students to interact more in the larger campus culture. Both professors and the larger Biola student body say that they would enjoy interacting with the Korean students more, but that they do not feel comfortable interrupting a group of students speaking Korean. Korean students say that it would be very strange to speak to another Korean in English, so they continue interacting in Korean. The large number of Korean students both at Biola and in Los Angeles means that there are many students who have an extensive circle of Korean friends and family as well as church and ministry responsibilities. ELSP offers training on both sides. Workshops have been offered to faculty and staff to give tips for interacting with NNS students and to give staff and faculty time to communicate with students. ELSP instructors encourage students to speak English in the classroom and during breaks, and they provide activities where students interact on campus. They encourage students not to wait till their English is better but to get involved in English-medium activities now, often assigning them as homework. These activities have included attending special lectures on and off campus, participating in local Bible studies, and hiking with a group that includes native speakers.

Conclusion

In conclusion, ELSP offers Talbot's NNS students an opportunity not only to prepare for the academic demands of seminary study in English, but also the opportunity to integrate into the larger university community. There are challenges when integrating seminarians and other majors in the same language classes and challenges when integrating NNS students on a larger campus, but the myriad of resources offered by a language institute in a university-based seminary provide good opportunities for meeting these challenges.

Chapter 2

Starting at Zero: A Two-year English Preparation Program for Polish Seminary Students

Carole Poleski
poleski@ili.net

Carole Poleski has been teaching ESL at Saints Cyril and Methodius Seminary in Orchard Lake, Michigan since 1996. She has a master's degree in TESOL. Her research and presentation interests are grammar pedagogy and second language speaking skills.

The need to recruit more Catholic priests in the U.S. is what originally led to the ESL program at Saints Cyril and Methodius Seminary in Orchard Lake, a suburb of Detroit, Michigan. It started from a personal connection between a Polish priest on the faculty and his contacts back in Poland and has resulted in a steady stream of young Polish men coming to the seminary since the mid-1980s. Since then, the network of contacts with Polish bishops and seminary rectors has grown steadily. Students spend up to two years concentrating on English and acculturation in the ESL program before beginning their seminary studies. Until about eight years ago, many were true beginners; however, as more English courses have become available in Poland, their level of English proficiency has risen.

Prospective students must be high school graduates who have completed two years of philosophy studies. Most students in each year's incoming class are between twenty-two and twenty-five years of age and have completed some course work in Polish seminaries; however, older candidates and those with different educational backgrounds (e.g., university) are also encouraged to apply and have often been accepted. Students are able to transfer a portion of their credits from theology studies in Poland to this seminary. Depending on the number of transferable credits, students' time at the seminary generally ranges from three to six years, including one to four semesters of ESL study.

Program

For almost twenty years the seminary provided ESL instruction to all incoming Polish seminarians. The classes, for the most part, took true beginners to a level where they could score 525 on the paper-based TOEFL in a two-year period. About four years ago, the seminary administrators began exploring the possibility of creating a house of formation in Krakow, Poland to prepare prospective candidates for the seminary in Michigan. The advantages of this new feeder school approach are many: lower costs of room, board, and tuition; time for formation faculty to observe the candidates as they participate in the program before coming to a foreign country; and time for students to learn more about our seminary and prayerfully consider their option to leave their homeland. The plan is for students to complete one year of EFL studies in Krakow, and then come to Michigan for a year of ESL followed by matriculation in the Master of Divinity program. We have now had three incoming classes made up of the students from Krakow and other applicants. Overall, the program in Krakow has been deemed beneficial to the students and the seminary, and it is expected to grow as the number of applicants increase. One sign of its success was that the original formation house was promoted to seminary status this past year and has moved to larger quarters. It is now known as Saints Cyril and Methodius Seminary of Krakow.

With all of these changes, the ESL program at the seminary in Michigan is still flexibly designed to accommodate the varying proficiency levels among each entering class. The fifteen newcomers who started this year, for example, included students at three levels. Currently there are seven beginners, four intermediates, and five high-intermediates. Each group stays together for all their classes, which are designed specifically for their level of proficiency.

Placement

Several placement tools are used at the beginning of each academic year when new students arrive at the seminary in Michigan. All students (first- and second-year) are required to take a standardized test. The Michigan

Placement Test was used extensively in the past, but we now use an institutional version of the paper-based TOEFL. Students are required to have a minimum TOEFL score of 525 before they can enter the theology program and do part-time theology and part-time ESL. They need a score of 550 before they can exit ESL classes altogether. In addition to the TOEFL, new (first-year) students provide a writing sample (thirty minutes), do a picture-based oral language skills test (ten minutes), and participate in a brief, audio-recorded oral interview with an ESL instructor. Using these measures, the ESL faculty group students according to their English proficiency levels.

Curriculum

At each level of full-time ESL, courses are offered in Reading/Writing (eight hours a week), Grammar (six hours a week), and Listening/Speaking (six hours a week). These twenty class hours a week are required for all full-time ESL students. Students are assigned an average of one-half to one hour of homework per class contact hour. During the second year (or second semester for intermediate level), an optional one to two hours of TOEFL preparation class is added.

Currently, with students at three levels, three full-time instructors share the teaching load; each instructor teaches twenty hours of classes per week. All instructors have the M.A. TESOL degree and a rich variety of teaching experience in the U.S. and other countries.

Grammar

The grammar classes use the *Grammar in Context* and *Grammar Form and Function* series of textbooks. In addition to the textbook and workbook, instructors use authentic materials such as newspapers, magazines, book excerpts, short stories, songs, or video to present or review grammar points.

Reading/Writing

The reading curriculum teaches the usual reading skills such as distinguishing main ideas and details, prediction, and inference, with special attention given to helping students learn to state and support personal opinions in response to the readings. Vocabulary development is particularly emphasized in this class, with attention paid to Latin and Greek roots, word parts and word families. Textbooks include the series *All About the USA, Strategic Reading, Vocabulary Mastery*, and *Improving Vocabulary Skills*. Higher-level classes read *The Book of Virtues*, and for all classes supplemental materials are also brought in from newspapers, magazines, the Internet, short stories, speeches, and poetry. In addition to assignments from the main textbook, students are required to read about topics of particular interest to them and follow up with oral and/or written reports. A certain amount of extensive reading, beyond the normal daily assignments, is also required for some classes. For this purpose, the campus library and the ESL office maintain a stock of trade books, religious books and level-adapted English classics, although students may choose any other English print materials they wish to read. American culture provides much of the context for the reading classes. In the higher-level classes, English language films are also assigned to be viewed as homework, in order to enrich the treatment of cultural topics and as sources for discussion, writing, and further reading.

The early writing classes start with English sentence structure and move to paragraphs and simple essays. At higher levels, students write essays to respond to a reading, to express an opinion, or to argue a point. Standard North American paragraph and essay organization are taught and practiced extensively. The complete development of ideas is a focus at this level. Paraphrasing and academic reference conventions are also covered. Frequently used textbooks include *Introduction to Academic Writing*, *Great Paragraphs*, and *Great Essays*.

Academic reading and writing skills are probably the biggest teaching challenges, and among the last that the students acquire. The Internet is a very popular source of information, and the ease of cutting and pasting a document makes it altogether too easy to succumb to the temptation to plagiarize, even without the intention to do so. Seminary faculty encourage students to read extensively and to respond to what they read in discussion and writing, but in the modern world of instant communication and information retrieval, it is not common for students to want to settle down with a good book.

Listening/Speaking

Because these students are preparing for parish ministry and not just learning English for academic purposes, the development of their oral skills is an important part of the program. Early in the program, the focus is on the social use of English in conversations. Students listen to and practice using greetings, explanations, apologies, questions and answers, directions, descriptions, and other functions. Television and radio are also used occasionally to give the students practice in understanding such common programs as news and weather reports. Academic listening is introduced using recorded lectures in ESL textbooks such as the *Open Forum* and

Panorama series, and instructor-created materials using National Public Radio broadcasts. English idioms are taught when they naturally arise in class, and in structured lessons from the textbooks *All Clear* and *In the Know*. The instructors encourage class discussions and assign oral reports on various topics to give the students practice in speaking in front of groups. Higher-level classes practice note-taking and critical thinking exercises on academic and cultural topics. At every level, students are required to give weekly oral scripture readings and reflections in class. Instructors evaluate these presentations using a rubric based on the speaker's use of grammar, syntax, vocabulary, and pronunciation.

Instruction in pronunciation includes a needs-based focus on individual phonemes in addition to practice with rhythm, stress, and intonation. Oral presentation skills are practiced, with special attention to eye contact, volume, and rate of speech.

TOEFL Preparation
At all levels above beginning, students prepare for the TOEFL using the *Longman TOEFL* preparation textbook. Some class time is devoted to this, and students may also practice TOEFL skills outside of class with the CD-ROM that accompanies the textbook, as well as test preparation materials available in the library and on the Internet.

The TOEFL is administered by ESL instructors in August, December, and April. This schedule gives students several opportunities to achieve the required score in order to begin theological studies in September or January.

Materials Summary
As noted above, we use mostly standard, published ESL materials. These serve the purpose of taking our students from a beginning English level to a level at which they can study theology and begin their local ministry. Though no theology-specific ESL materials are used, instructors often use articles or excerpts from books that deal with religious beliefs, prayer, and spirituality as a basis for discussions and ESL assignments.

Other Resources
The seminary has a Sony language lab that is used regularly by each class. Lab activities include writing with Microsoft Word; recording passages to be evaluated for pronunciation; listening to radio or recorded texts; use of the Rosetta Stone program; and the use of interactive ESL websites, which are popular among students for the game-like instruction and additional

practice they offer. In addition, we have a computer based English course, ELLIS, which enables students to review and study grammar, listening, functional language, and pronunciation at their own pace. The ELLIS computer is located in the main seminary building and is available to students at any time, but the language lab is available only during scheduled class times.

Extracurricular Activities

ESL instructors are available to meet with students individually, either for regularly scheduled tutoring sessions or occasional appointments. The instructors organize field trips, including visits to Catholic and Protestant churches, a synagogue, museums, a courtroom, restaurants, and the University of Michigan campus. Instructors have also accompanied students to concerts, movies, and the theater.

One of the biggest challenges to learning English at the seminary is that students speak Polish with each other, most of the resident priests, and many of the campus staff. The students spend most of their time on campus, which in fact could almost be considered an EFL, not an ESL, environment. The transition to English is gradual. In order to increase student contact with English speakers, certain extracurricular activities are offered.

Conversation Partners: First-year students are assigned conversation partners at a nearby retirement home for members of the order of the Sisters of Mercy. They meet with their partners one hour weekly throughout the school year and are encouraged to view their participation as a form of ministry. Many students develop lasting friendships with their conversation partners and stay in touch with them long after the program ends.

Field Education: During their final semester of ESL, students take the seminary's introductory Field Education course. The course entails four or five class meetings and a supervised field placement once a week in a nursing home, hospital, jail, soup kitchen, or food pantry. At the end of the semester, students prepare a theological reflection on their field education experience.

Summer Placements: Students are usually affiliated with a U.S. diocese by the end of their first year in Michigan. Each student is required to spend about ten weeks in his diocese during the summer. The details of their assignments are worked out by their diocesan vocation directors in collaboration with the seminary administrators, and these assignments tend to vary greatly among dioceses and parishes. However, the students usually experience increased contact with English speakers and American parish life. Thus, by the time they return to the seminary for their next academic year, most of them have made notable progress in English skills, acculturation, and priestly formation.

Conclusion

The ESL program at Saints Cyril and Methodius Seminary is an example of how seminaries need to remain responsive to rapidly changing contexts. When the Polish students first arrived in the 1980s, the program had to cope with the challenge of preparing complete beginners for both academic study and parish ministry in a short time. When the Krakow program started in 2005, the ESL program had to adjust and accommodate students at a variety of levels. The Polish language environment on the seminary campus remains one of the biggest challenges to the students' acquisition of English, yet the extracurricular activities, including summer placement in an American parish, help counter that. Four semesters is a relatively short period for full-time English instruction, yet students are able to make the transition to a new social and academic culture, a new model for the priesthood, and the new language in which they will fulfill their promise of service to the American church.

ESL Texts Used in this Program

Bennett, W. (1996). *The book of virtues.* New York: Simon and Schuster.

Blackwell, A. & T. Naber. (2008). *Open forum: Academic listening and speaking.* Oxford: Oxford University Press.

Broukal, M. (2002). *Grammar form and function.* New York: McGraw Hill.

Broukal, M. (2007). *All about the USA: A cultural reader.* White Plains, NY: Pearson Longman.

Elbaum, S. (2005). *Grammar in context* (4th ed.). Boston: Heinle.

Flynn, K. (2006). *Panorama: Building perspective through reading.* Oxford: Oxford University Press.

Folse, K. et al. (2003). *Great paragraphs* (2nd ed.). Boston: Heinle.

Folse, K. et al. (2003). *Great essays* (2nd ed.). Boston: Heinle.

Fragiadakis, H. (2006). *All clear: Idioms in context* (3rd ed.). Boston:Heinle.

Leaney, C. (2005). *In the know: Understanding and using idioms* Cambridge: Cambridge University Press.

Mohr, S. (2002). *Improving vocabulary skills.* West Berlin: NJ: Townsend Press.

Oshima, A. & A. Hogue. (2006). *Introduction to academic writing* (3rd ed.) White Plains, NY: Pearson Longman.

Richards, J. (2003). *Strategic reading.* Cambridge: Cambridge University Press.

Wells, L. (2007). *Vocabulary mastery.* Ann Arbor: University of Michigan Press.

Chapter 3

Individualized Support for ESL Students During Theological Studies

Amy Spencer
spencera@ohiodominican.edu

Amy Spencer taught at the Pontifical College Josephinum School of
Theology from 1991 to 2004; she is currently Director of the Academic
Resource Center at Ohio Dominican University.

Some seminaries do not have enough students at the same proficiency level to warrant full classes. This chapter describes what the ESL program at the Pontifical College Josephinum was like in the early 2000s and shows how one instructor can meet the varied language needs of international seminarians studying in the U.S. This Roman Catholic seminary located in a suburb of Columbus, Ohio has a graduate school of theology with an average annual enrollment of seventy-five men preparing for the priesthood. Some transfer in at upper levels; most start with first-year classes. A quarter to a third of these are non-native speakers of English, from nations such as Latvia, Poland, Uganda, Tanzania, Nigeria, Mexico, Venezuela, Myanmar, Korea, and Vietnam.

Half of these students are studying for dioceses in the U.S.; the others will return to ministry in their native countries. In order to complete their academic work, students need a high degree of proficiency in reading and writing as well as listening and note-taking. Those who stay in the U.S., in addition, need near native oral fluency, so accurate pronunciation is a major concern for them. Admission to the School of Theology requires a TOEFL score of 500; students scoring between 450 and 500 are conditionally accepted, with the expectation that they will take a reduced course load, supplemented with ESL instruction. Non-native speakers who score 500 or above may elect to meet with the ESL instructor for tutorials.

All non-native speakers meet with the instructor[1] for an in-house evaluation of their language proficiency. Students produce a writing sample based on a short philosophical article, complete a brief assessment of grammar, and record a text for the purposes of diagnosing their oral proficiency. In addition, they are interviewed to gather background information and to inquire about their concerns regarding studying in English. At this time, students are also given the option of being matched with an American family who will provide social support and intercultural communication opportunities.

The program is individualized to meet the specific needs of incoming students. Each student receives from one to three hours of individual tutoring weekly to support them in their theology classes. Most students meet with the ESL instructor regularly for three or four semesters and thereafter only stop by periodically with questions about a paper or project. Depending on the students' need, tutoring is provided in study skills, pronunciation, grammar, computer skills, citation style, library research, and so on. To be effective in supporting the students in this range of topics, the instructor meets regularly with the library staff and the English and technology departments for purposes of locating and using resources, and with the theology faculty to make sure students are meeting their expectations.

Some years the incoming group of international students is homogeneous enough to warrant group instruction in classes, such as "Information Processing: Listening, Note-taking, and Reading," or "Pronunciation." The class content includes both ESL texts and supplements geared for a seminary audience (e.g., Rosser 1996, Sparough 1988) and assignments are linked to what students are doing in their theology courses.

International students make up a significant proportion of the Pontifical College Josephinum School of Theology students, so it is important to serve them well. Assisting them in critical reading, lecture note-taking, and pronunciation by means of content that is closely allied to their theological studies is a priority. At the same time, they are often

---

1   The ESL teacher at this time had an academic home in the Department of English in the Josephinum's College of Liberal Arts; her role was ESL program developer, coordinator and sole instructor.

so varied in terms of their placement in theological studies and their English proficiency that an individualized tutorial program is the only answer. Such a program is made possible by a versatile ESL teacher and cooperation across departmental lines.

ESL Texts Used in this Program

Rosser, A. (1996). *A Well-trained tongue: Formation in the ministry of reader.* Chicago: Liturgy Training Publications.

Sparough, J. M. (1988). *Lector training program: This is the word of the Lord.* Chicago: Liturgy Training Publications.

Chapter 4

One Body, One Spirit: The Integrity of Institutional Goals and Instructional Decisions

Leslie Altena
latena@wts.edu

Leslie Altena is the director of the Center for Theological Writing at Westminster Theological Seminary in Philadelphia, Pennsylvania. She also teaches courses in second language acquisition, second language writing, and curriculum design at the University of Pennsylvania and Temple University.

The purpose of this article is to examine how institutional goals interrelate with instructional decisions in an advanced theological writing class for ESL students.[1] I give examples of how changes were made in the curriculum in response to shifts in the literacy goals of administrators, faculty, and students at Westminster Theological Seminary, located in Philadelphia, Pennsylvania. I try to describe this interrelationship in terms of principles for the design of second language writing curricula on the institutional as well as the classroom level. I begin with some background about the seminary and then relate three key incidents that show how seminary goals relate to teaching practice. My hope is that this discussion will help others

---

1   An earlier version of this paper, "Institutional Goals and ESL Writing Instruction: The Case of Advanced Theological Writing at Westminster Seminary," was presented at the Christian Educators in Language Teaching conference in Long Beach, California, on March 30, 2004.

design theological writing instruction that responds to the unique needs of administrators, faculty, and students in their settings.

Advanced Theological Writing at Westminster Theological Seminary

Westminster Theological Seminary enrolls between 700 and 800 students on its main campus and its associated programs. Founded on the principles of the Westminster Confession, this conservative Reformed seminary offers courses in apologetics, systematics, biblical studies/hermeneutics, church history, and practical theology. Students from approximately fifty nations and one hundred denominations pursue master's and doctoral degrees; international students comprise about eleven percent of the total student population. International students are required to meet TOEFL minimums to enter the seminary: 570 (88 iBT) for master's-level tracks, and 600 (100 iBT) for Th.M. and Ph.D. tracks. All students whose scores meet these minimums but fall below 640 (111 iBT) are required to enroll in the Advanced Theological Writing (ATW) course. The Dean of International Students explains the rationale for the course, focusing on the students' desire for academic achievement and the faculty's need for help in fairly evaluating second language writing:

> We require the advanced theological writing course because we have determined that if students' scores fall below the TOEFL score they do not do well in the coursework, primarily because of the way they communicate in their papers, making it difficult for professors to evaluate them. We want a course focused on writing because that is really where students are evaluated here, in both test-taking and the papers. That is where they have the most problems, and faculty run into frustrations. The teaching is very didactic here, so students are not required to speak often. The issue for the faculty is the writing. (Patty Comber, personal communication, March 2004)

The ATW class in its present form provides an intensive introduction to theological genres; practice in advanced grammar using authentic theological texts; instruction in achieving coherence; instruction on paragraph and essay organization; practice with critical thinking; guidance in revision and editing; and review of documentation practices.[2] In addition,

---

2   In designing a theological writing course, I have found it helpful to consult texts on language curriculum design such as Brown (1995) and Woodward (2000) as well as guides to second language writing pedagogy such as Ferris and Hedgcock (2005), Grabe and Kaplan (1996), Hyland (2003), Leki (1992;

the ATW instructor is responsible for providing feedback on grammatical errors on all papers written by the students for the other seminary courses in which they are enrolled during the semester they are in ATW.

Curriculum Design Options for Advanced Theological Writing

To examine the mix of institutional and classroom issues affecting curriculum design, a model based on Cumming (2003) and Richards and Rodgers (1982) is helpful. In terms of the institutional level, according to Cumming (2003), writing courses are usually delivered in one of three basic formats: independent focus on writing, partially integrated focus that links writing and reading, or fully integrated focus that combines speaking, listening, reading, and writing. Course goals tend to fall into two categories: development of specific professional competencies or general improvement in academic language, style, self-expression, composing ability, and rhetoric. The conceptualization of what writing is may also vary from personal expression to composing processes to mastery of a certain genre, and so on.

Decisions made at the classroom or instructional level are described succinctly in Richards and Rodgers' (1982) model of approach, design, and procedure. *Approach* is the assumptions, beliefs, and theories which form the foundation for instruction. Ideally, there is a match between the instructor's approach and the institution's conceptualization of writing. For example, both may view writing as a set of processes. *Design* flows out of approach and includes content (including selection and sequencing of course objectives), learner roles, teacher roles, and instructional materials. *Procedure* includes the specific techniques, practices, and activities used in the classroom. Examples of procedures in theological writing include answering analytical questions about a sample apologetics paper, researching how a grammatical form is used in theological writing, or carrying out the steps of biblical exegesis.

In what follows, I use these concepts from Cumming and Richard and Rodgers to trace how change happened on the institutional and classroom level. As adjunct faculty members, second language writing instructors at seminaries can become isolated from institutional level decisions about curriculum while at the same time, as the "language experts" in their context, they are given broad decision making power

---

1998), Raimes (1983), Silva (1990), and Williams (2005). The latter provide research-based approaches to teaching second language writing, specific instructional techniques, materials, course outlines, assignments, and so on.

over the instructional level. In fact, the institutional and instructional levels are integrally related: change initiated in one level exerts pressure for change in the other, as the following narrative of the development the Advanced Theological Writing course illustrates.

The Original Course: English Writing Skills

The problem of understanding and fairly evaluating ESL student's written work was the reason for creating the English Writing Skills (EWS) course in 1987 as a non-credit, required course for entering international students (F1 or J1 visa status) whose TOEFL scores fell below a 650 minimum; the course was to be taken during the first semester and repeated, if necessary, until passed. A faculty member could also require a student to enroll. The catalog description of EWS from the 1990s read:

> A non-credit course offered each semester. Required of entering international students . . . This course will focus on basic English writing skills, will require several short writing assignments, and will provide grammatical and syntactical correction for all papers, sermons and presentations required in regular seminary courses.

As interpreted by the original instructor, there were four goals for the course: (1) acquaint international students with the definition of plagiarism and avoid it; (2) provide grammatical correction of all papers; (3) provide practice in composing paragraphs; (4) give students information about Western educational expectations as well as supply informative feedback on their writing. To fulfill the requirement for correction, the students were asked to write a first draft of their course papers and submit them to the EWS instructor's mailbox several days in advance of the due date.

In Cumming's (2003) terms, the initial course format for EWS was *independent* and the course goal was *general academic competence*. By improving the academic competence of students, the faculty members' desire to understand and fairly evaluate student work would be addressed, as would the difficult and time-consuming problem of plagiarized papers. Another important concept in curriculum design, the guiding conceptualization of writing, in this case was *writing as grammatical structure*, with the supporting conceptualizations of writing as composing, and writing as conforming to genre expectations, described broadly as "Western." Remarkable in this earliest picture of theological writing curriculum is the lack of specificity for *theological* writing. The course was seen by administrators as remedial

English, and its purpose was to cover material that all students should have mastered before matriculation into seminary.

Drawing on Richards and Rogers to understand the dynamics of classroom instruction, the *approach* included grammatical correctness, and the theory of teaching was controlled composition as well as correction and practice. As for *design*, the teacher's role was to be the source of knowledge, including knowledge of academic writing standards and knowledge about the English language. The teacher provided correction, and the learners were recipients and implementers of this knowledge. The instructional materials—including excerpts from Turabian's *A Manual for Writers of Term Papers, Theses, and Dissertations* and paragraph outlines—supported students to work independently and enabled them to analyze and structure their writing.

When I started to teach the EWS course in 1994, I saw a strong grammatical focus was important to the institution, but I also needed to consider my own conceptualization of writing, which included text types and the composing process. My theory of learning writing included correction, and thus was in line with institutional policy to correct papers, but for me the effectiveness of correction was explained by the cognitive theory of the role of feedback in language learning; in other words, my emphasis on correction had less to do with behavior modification and more to do with the ability of correction to facilitate the students' noticing of linguistic features.

In sum, I introduced a change in course design through changing the *approach* to classroom instruction. At the same time, I continued to work under the original institutional goal, that of improving the students' general academic competence by addressing basic writing skills, short writing assignments and providing correction. Being new, I had no experience working with administrators to change the course goal or format. The resulting tension between goal, format and teaching method was not resolved until issues surrounding the course were dealt with at an institutional level, as described in the next section.

My change in approach led to changes in classroom *procedure*. For example, to help students understand the concerns of their readers, I assigned the presentation of an article or book chapter written by a faculty member. In addition to teaching paragraph structure, I began teaching summary writing, personal response, exegesis, and critical thinking. I designed assignments that were shorter versions of different theological genres. This led to changes in course *design*, as I viewed learners as linguistic and theological resources for each other, and myself as a facilitator as well as a source of knowledge. I introduced reading assignments as well, including samples of theological writing collected from students, professors, and professional journals.

As a result of these changes, I quickly found the job of teaching EWS overwhelming and unmanageable. Upon reflection, I can see that the reason I was overwhelmed was that I had tried to change the course on the level of instructional method without also working on the institutional level to redefine the course goal. I was trying to teach a course that was directed toward general academic competence to satisfy the institutional needs, in addition to one directed toward specific theological competence. I was striving to accomplish all of this in addition to correcting all the students' papers for their other courses, making my job nearly impossible to carry out in a reasonable amount of time.

The struggle took me repeatedly to the academic dean's office from 1994 through 1999, to report that I had too many outside papers to correct. In any single semester, I could have over one hundred papers of varying lengths, and with full enrollment, it could take me 250-300 hours per semester to teach EWS and correct all the written work. I became bewildered and discouraged by the charge to teach writing as an adjunct faculty member *and* do so much correction of a variety of course papers. Through talks with the academic dean, I also became acutely aware of the core purpose of the EWS course, to accommodate faculty needs to grade the papers fairly, and I also began to argue for more effective writing support so that students would really learn to write and not need so much outside correction.

Discussions surrounding EWS eventually involved the academic dean, dean of students, and the admissions office in such questions as, Is the seminary in the business of language education? How extensive should language education be? This debate continued for several years, with some investigation of area programs and several proposals made for multi-level language education at the seminary. No substantive changes were made, however, until there was a student-led reaction to EWS and the language policies of the institution in the spring of 1999.

1999-2000: Plagiarism and the TOEFL Requirement

In the spring 1999 semester, I had eleven students enrolled in the class, and nine of them were plagiarizing in their theological papers regularly. Now, in addition to my continued struggle with an overwhelming schedule of correction, I spent time with them individually, trying to teach them summary and research skills with the result that the students as a group petitioned the faculty, complaining that the course was all about plagiarism and not enough about grammar; they also objected that the TOEFL requirement for exemption from the course was unreasonably high.

In response, a committee of faculty members and administrators was formed to discuss English writing support at the seminary. Interestingly, the discussion soon focused on the TOEFL *entrance* requirement. Some committee members took the position that high scores required for admission[3] were actually keeping otherwise qualified students out, while others argued that high scores protected students with insufficient language preparation from trying to come in and take on too much. Those who took the former position also supported lowering the entrance requirement and increasing language support for students at the seminary, while those who took the latter position wanted to keep the scores as they had been and focus on the seminary goals of theological training. The latter group even proposed increasing the entrance requirements, thereby communicating that students should enter seminary with a high level of English writing ability, or be prepared to learn writing elsewhere if the single EWS course could not provide enough support. My contribution to the committee was to collect information about TOEFL policies at eleven comparable seminaries and to carry out a pilot validity study that looked at how students' TOEFL and TWE scores compared with ratings of the writing quality in samples from their theological course papers.

In the end, the TOEFL entrance requirements to the seminary were preserved, but the minimums for the course exemption were lowered slightly based on the analysis of writing samples. In the process, the institutional literacy goals were questioned and interpreted: The seminary's purpose was basically theological, and it was not prepared to offer more extended language support, or to lower entrance requirements, as a means to invite more international students to enter. Another result of this process was that the administration shifted its position toward

---

3   As explained above, the minimum TOEFL score for admission was 570 (88 iBT) for master's-level tracks, and 600 (100 iBT) for Th.M. and Ph.D. tracks. In spring 1999, the score for exemption from the ATW course was still 650.

greater literacy support: they funded a teaching assistant to help with correction, freeing up my time to organize and train seminary approved editors whom the students could contract with to give feedback on their work once the students had passed the required writing class. Finally, through what had been at times a painful, time-consuming process, I learned to understand seminary goals, contribute even as an adjunct instructor to policy decisions, and develop better working relationships with administrators and faculty members.

The *design* and *procedure* of my course again changed. I started listening to my students more carefully, and I gave them a greater role in designing the class. In response to their requests, for example, I began using more traditional materials, such as excerpts from workbooks, and again in response to their request, I made grammar instruction prominent on the syllabus. In response to students' feelings about plagiarism, I began framing my instruction on summary and synthesis as methods to avoid plagiarism. I also increased my use of sample papers connected with their theological assignments. Now that I had an assistant, I was able to spend the time to develop authentic materials. In sum, the shift on the classroom level that had made the class overwhelming to teach was now being supported administratively, and the change was beginning to be reflected on the institutional level in conception of the course goal as specific competence in theological writing.

2003-2004: A Charge of Discrimination

In the above two cases, change on the classroom and institutional levels came about because of feedback from administrators and from students as a group. In this last example, however, change came from one student's objection to the institution's literacy policy and one of the course writing assignments.

In the fall of 2003, a student was asked to take the class who did not feel she belonged in it. She did not pass the exemption exam, and went to the dean of international students with a strong protest against her exam results and the writing assignment. The first day, to teach about audience and purpose, I had asked students to write out a prayer about their seminary work and contrast that with how they would talk to their friends about the same topic. I explicitly stated that this was not a graded assignment, but was given because the activity was familiar and clearly shows how word and topic choice are tied to audience and purpose. However, the student took offense at what she saw as an overly personal assignment that was inappropriate to grade, and viewed the request as insensitive to her cultural views on what should be private and personal.

She linked her reactions to charges that the seminary discriminates against international students through requiring the EWS course.

Again I landed in the dean's office, talking over policies as a result of this student's grievance. It once again raised the question of language requirements at the seminary and how well the course serves those requirements, this time with respect to fairness—should all students be required to pass a writing test? One of the important questions raised was, what message is the seminary sending to international students about its attitude toward them, by the way the descriptions are worded and the class conducted? It was another test of institutional goals and their implementation.

The result of this round of changes was that the Dean of International Students, in consultation with me, made a revision in the catalog description and changed the name of the course to Advanced Theological Writing. Where the earlier course description, quoted above, sounds critical of the students, arising as it does from a conception that the course is remedial (and ideally would not be necessary), this version is meant to soothe and compliment the reader:

> The purpose of this course is to equip students to write theological papers clearly and accurately in English. Topics covered include the thesis; overall organization and paragraph structure in theological writing; styles of writing critical reviews, exegesis, and research papers; summary, paraphrase, quotation, and documentation forms; vocabulary development; and advanced English grammar.

Elsewhere, the catalog describes the course in this way:

> The ability to produce quality written work in English is expected of all Westminster degree recipients. International students with extensive English language training, as well as those with advanced degrees in other professional fields, find it advantageous to learn the expectations of American academic writing; study the special features of theological genres; and receive feedback on their linguistic accuracy. The course PT 031p or PT 033p Advanced Theological Writing is provided as a support for these students.

As a result of institutional initiative this time, the approach, design, and procedure of the class changed as I tried harder to convey respect and welcome the students by treating them as high academic achievers.

In terms of *design* and *procedure*, I used a genre-based *approach* (Hyland, 2003), holding students responsible, for example, for analyzing genres and relating that analysis to their own writing. I kept the grammar workbook because students liked it, but I began to use it more as a resource for individual students to work on their particular grammar issues. I also taught the students some language acquisition theory, so they would understand how my feedback was intended to support their language development, and that they would do well to study their patterns of error and compare their own language to the target language. The change in design included a change in learner roles from students needing remediation to sophisticated learners, who could draw on their cognitive and analytical abilities to support their language learning.

Conclusion

The development of theological writing instruction over the seventeen-year period described in this article began at the institutional level and spread to the classroom (top-down) as well as beginning from classroom and moving to the institutional level (bottom-up). After the initial estab-lish-ment of the course (top-down), the change in instructors brought change in classroom methods, which in turn put pressure on administrators to develop their views of how the course fit into the mission of the semina-ry (bottom-up). In the final example, we saw that an individual student's pressure on administration to change (bottom-up) brought further change to the classroom (top-down).

Change came about as administrators, faculty and students began to understand each other's purposes more clearly. No one operated alone; rather, change in one area exerted pressure on the others. As a new adjunct faculty member I had to discover that changes that I wanted to see in instruction could not be made entirely on my own and still be manageable; rather, I had to learn about my place in the larger system, lessons that were at times difficult and time-consuming. Experiences such as those described here, however, illustrate the integrity of the relationship between institutional and classroom levels in designing a theological writing curriculum.

ESL Texts Used in this Program

Brown, J. D. (1995). *The elements of language curriculum: A systematic approach to program development*. Boston: Heinle & Heinle.

Cumming, A. (2003). Experienced ESL/EFL writing instructors' conceptualizations of their teaching: Curriculum options and their implications. In B. Kroll (Ed.), *Exploring the dynamics of second language writing* (pp. 71-92). Cambridge: Cambridge University Press.

Ferris, D., & Hedgcock, J. S. (2005). *Teaching ESL composition: Purpose, process, and practice* (2nd ed.). Mahwah, NJ: Erlbaum.

Grabe, W., & Kaplan, R. B. (1996). *Theory and practice of writing: An applied linguistic perspective.* London: Longman.

Hyland, K. (2003). *Second language writing.* Cambridge: Cambridge University Press.

Leki, I. (1992). *Understanding ESL writers: A guide for teachers.* Portsmouth, NH: Boynton/Cook, Reed Elsevier.

Leki, I. (1998). *Academic writing: Exploring processes and strategies* (2nd ed.). Cambridge: Cambridge University Press.

Long M. H. & J. C. Richards (Eds.) *Methodology in TESOL: A book of readings* (pp. 145-157). Boston, MA: Heinle.

Raimes, A. (1983). *Techniques in teaching writing.* New York: Oxford University Press.

Richards, J. C. & R. Rodgers. (1987). Method: Approach, design, and procedure. In M. H. Long & J. C. Richards (Eds.) *Methodology in TESOL: A book of readings* (pp. 145-157). Boston, MA: Heinle.

Silva, T. (1990). Second language composition instruction: Developments, issues and directions in ESL. In B. Kroll (Ed.), *Second language writing: Research insights for the classroom* (pp. 11-23). Cambridge: Cambridge University Press.

Turabian, Kate. (2007). *A manual for writers of research papers, theses, and dissertations.* 7th ed. Chicago: University of Chicago Press.

Williams, J. (2005). *Teaching writing in second and foreign language classrooms.* Boston: McGraw-Hill.

Woodward, T. (2001). *Planning lessons and courses: Designing sequences of work for the language classroom.* Cambridge: Cambridge University Press.

Chapter 5

Enculturation to American Academic Expectations: The Role of Peer Writing Tutor Programs

Jennifer Mawhorter
jmawhorter@cst.edu

Jennifer Mawhorter is Director of the Writing Center and ESL
at Claremont School of Theology. Previously, she taught ESL to
international teaching assistants at the University of California,
Riverside. She received her M.Sc. in Psycholinguistics from the
University of Edinburgh and her M.A. in Teaching English as a Second
Language from the University of Texas, Austin.

The study of theology involves a great deal of writing; thus, helping all
students, both native and non-native English speakers, with their writing
is a concern to many seminaries. I teach ESL and direct the writing center
at Claremont School of Theology in California where every year all new
students, both ESL and native English-speaking, are asked to write an academic essay during orientation. The purpose of this essay exam is to identify
students who may need extra help meeting expectations for graduate-level
writing. In reading the essays written by incoming international students,
one's attention may be drawn to surface errors, such as word choice and
article errors, but in fact the needs of the international students are not so
different from those of the native speaking students: both need to learn to
come up with original, appropriate arguments, supported with examples
and evidence. The biggest challenge for many students is understanding

what is expected in each discipline and learning to develop a clear, arguable thesis to fit each assignment, rather than merely summarizing what sources have to say. This chapter addresses ways of helping students with that challenge.

Our international student population is overwhelmingly Korean, with central Africans and Pacific Islanders making up the majority of the other international students. Many have never written a paper, a few have written research papers that bring together and summarize sources without taking a personal stance, and none have written the kinds of focused, thesis-driven papers that are typically required by American professors at graduate-level theological schools. Even for American students, the genres are new: reflection papers, book reviews, exegesis papers, text analysis papers from original (often ancient) sources, ethical arguments, and self-evaluations of counseling, leadership, and teaching skills. However, at least the American students have written many papers before and know, however incompletely, the basic structure of an academic paper with introduction, body, and conclusion. They know the meaning of common transition words even if they forget to use them. Most importantly, North American and most Western European students are accustomed to critiquing experts, pointing out flaws in arguments, marshalling evidence to support their own opinions, and taking a stance. Many international students have never been encouraged to develop their own opinions or rewarded for insightful criticism, highly valued in American academia.

When asked, the professors on our campus express two main pet peeves: papers with no thesis statements and plagiarism. Grading rubrics also reflect what American theology professors value. Comments like "An A Range Paper [includes] an interesting, incisive, focused thesis" (Suzanne Funsten, personal communication, 2005) and "Paper goes beyond the obvious aspects of the assignment . . . is ambitious, creative or original in its approach" (Duke Divinity School, 2003) underscore the need for international students to learn to think critically and put forward sophisticated arguments of their own. The prevalence of unintentional plagiarism by international students is partially a symptom of lack of original argument as well as failure to understand how to cite sources properly.

Peer Writing Tutors

So how can international students learn to be successful academic writers in American theological schools? In this chapter, I will argue that helping students develop their own voices can often best be furthered by individualized instruction and, with proper training, peer writing tutors can provide cost-effective academic support. While some graduate schools require a research/writing class for all students and some schools, including my institution, require international students to take academic writing classes along with regular coursework during their first semester, in my experience, most international students need individualized support to understand and meet expectations for graduate-level papers. Even with minimum iBT writing scores of twenty and concurrent academic writing classes, international students feel overwhelmed by unfamiliar demands.

Peer writing tutors can help internationals move through the academic maze[1] by working with students one-on-one to help them interpret assignments and find appropriate problems and questions to explore. Peer writing tutors can act as "cultural informants" to explain American academic values and writing conventions such as "intellectual property and attribution" (Gillespie & Learner, 2004). Tutors can gently tease out what students really think and help them move beyond summary to developing their own ideas. Socratic questioning and counter examples can help students refine ideas to come up with more nuanced statements. Praise from tutors who see beyond ESL errors to what students are trying to say helps students become more confident and develop their own voices.

International students need individual encouragement to engage in critical thinking about ideas and sources. Writing tutors can help students distinguish between higher order concerns and lower order concerns, global revision and sentence-level revision (see for example Gillespie & Olson, 2002, p. III.3.3; Ryan, 2002, p. 9-10). Tutors can help students see the importance of addressing issues of content and organization before addressing grammar and punctuation. Beyond this standard practice, I would like to suggest a few strategies and techniques that can help writing tutors work with international students to foster critical thinking.

Critical Thinking

One tool I discuss with writing tutors and students in my academic writing class is Bloom's taxonomy of learning objectives (see, for example, Kornuta

---

1   This term is from an international student I met with the day I was writing this. She was two weeks late turning in an assignment. She expressed her frustration with her writer's block and said she felt "like I am in a maze" when confronted with the complexity of meeting the professor's expectations for the assignment.

& Germaine, n.d.). Generally, graduate students in American theological schools are expected to go beyond knowledge and comprehension to application, analysis, synthesis, and evaluation. I train writing tutors to look beyond what is already present in the student's paper to what could be in the student's paper to demonstrate higher order thinking. Tutors are trained to read professors' assignments with students and help them see words and phrases in the assignments that point to expectations for higher order thinking. Tutors can generate questions, such as "How would you apply this to your field?" and "What do you think about this model?" to help students apply, evaluate, analyze, and synthesize what they've read.

One technique I teach students in my academic writing classes and writing tutors is to look for what Rosenwasser and Stephen (2003, p. 97-98) call "complicating evidence," evidence "for which your thesis does not account." Tutors can be trained to ask about complications and exceptions and listen to responses to help students reframe or reword arguments to "respond more fully to the evidence." Tutors may bring up objections ("So, what about . . . ?") that professors will also commonly articulate, giving students chances to refine their ideas before the final draft. Also, tutors can encourage students to look for sources that disagree with each other. The tendency for students once they find a topic is look for the required number of sources all supporting whatever argument they choose to make. Students wrongly focus on topic instead of argument, so often there is no overlap in areas of concern among the sources. Students should be encouraged to look for sources that disagree with each other and with the student's thesis, so students can successfully analyze the evidence for themselves and take a stand.

I also teach students and tutors techniques for making a thesis more specific to avoid overgeneralization. For example, replacing weak verbs, such as *be* or *have*, with more specific active verbs forces students to make a more forceful claim (Rosenwasser & Stephen, 2003, p. 129-131). Tutors can ask questions such as "What do you mean by x?" to help students replace broad noun phrases with more specific noun phrases. Sometimes it helps if students see examples of a hypothetical progression from bad thesis statements to better thesis statements for a specific assignment. For example, one of the first assignments new students face is a very short text analysis essay on Perpetua's 3rd century account of her martyrdom for the History of Christianity course. The tutors have a handout that defines a good thesis statement and a sequence of progressively better thesis statements, starting with the obvious, "In this paper, I will show that Perpetua was martyred because of her faith." One of the advantages of a writing center based in a theological school is that tutors have taken required first-year courses previously themselves, understand the struggle to come up with an original thesis for an ancient text, and are familiar with the kinds of arguments acceptable in the particular disciplines represented at the school.

Sometimes international students generate simplistic arguments for lack of facility with commonly used linguistic devices or academic hedges to qualify or limit the strength of a claim to only what can be supported by the evidence. Although some students pick up the attitude and language of skepticism, what Swales & Feak (2004) call being "confidently uncertain," from reading journal articles in their fields, the purpose of academic hedging and common modifications of verb and noun phrases to limit the scope of a claim should be taught explicitly (see, for example, Swales & Feak, p. 125-130; Hübler, 1983). Since writing tutors are usually good students academically, these devices come easily to them and they need to be made more explicitly aware of how they are used, so they can help international students employ them appropriately.

One of the easiest ways for non-experts to enter the academic conversation is to critique sources indirectly by pointing out what has been neglected or left out, or what should have been included, rather than directly pointing out where a source is wrong. Tutors can ask "how does this fit with your experience?" to help international students evaluate authorities in light of their own cultural, national, and personal contexts. Many international students have worked or volunteered in churches; tutors can solicit stories from students' experiences that help them critique or apply what they have read or heard in class. By acknowledging the students' prior experience, tutors empower students to value their own contributions to the academic discussion.

Empathy

Of course, it is intimidating to write in a foreign language. Peer writing tutors ideally also offer friendship and empathy for international students trying to meet the overwhelming demands of graduate school in a foreign country. Tutors are trained to ask and listen to how students are feeling before asking them what kind of help they want. Anxiety can be reduced when students realize that they are not alone, that tutors are there to help. Students who come from cultures where more emphasis is placed on oral rather than written tradition have the opportunity to think out loud and process ideas with a receptive audience. Tutors can also be trained to look for patterns of error and help students develop personal editing checklists to empower internationals to find and fix their most common errors. What if there is no source of this kind of help for non-native speaking students at your institution? How can ESL professionals, staff, and professors ensure that international students receive the support they need to succeed academically? Some might consider starting a writing center or peer writing tutor program on campus. With work/study money, ten hours of initial training, ongoing supervision, and office or library space, such a program requires little investment. The International Writing Centers Association (http://writingcenters.org) offers valuable resources for starting a writing center. While there seem to be no books specifically on writing for international theological students, Yaghjian (2006) offers insights into the theological writing process in general.

What if there is a writing center but it is not meeting the needs of theological students? Ask to meet with the director to share concerns. Almost all writing center directors are eager to establish alliances with specific departments and programs to better serve their clients. Perhaps meeting with writing tutors to explain expectations and demands on international students in the program will help tutors to tailor interactions with students to the specific context. Offering examples of syllabi and assignments to both directors and tutors will show willingness to go beyond merely demanding specialized services for theological students; it exemplifies cooperation in developing the best possible tutoring for all. A helpful resource might be "Writing Across Borders," a film in which international students explain in their own words the challenges they face in meeting the writing expectations of American academia (Robertson, 2005). Although not specific to theological education, the film generates sympathy and understanding for cultural differences in rhetorical expectations.

Finally, for theological education that is situated in contexts where neither of these solutions is practicable, online writing centers often offer resources and remote tutoring by online chat, telephone, VOIP, or email response. Contracting for such services might be the best solution. In addition, ESL professionals or sympathetic staff and faculty can participate in T.A. training to help teaching assistants work with international students.

In conclusion, well-trained peer writing tutors can offer invaluable support to international theological students. Professors and writing instructors often do not have enough time to work individually with students on every paper; frequently, international students do not understand the comments that teaching assistants and professors write on their papers. In a writing center, there is time allotted for students and tutors to question, listen, brainstorm, laugh, and cry. Since research has shown that timely, personalized feedback has a significant impact on writing ability (Harvard Writing Project, 2008), the more that international students receive feedback targeted specifically to their own ideas and written work, the more likely they are to make progress in confidently and creatively writing in their theological contexts.

ESL Texts Used in this Program

Duke Divinity School. (2003). Rubric for narrative evaluation. Retrieved August 20, 2009, from http://www.divinity.duke.edu/docs/ctw/grading_rubric.pdf.

Gillespie, P. & Lerner, N. (2004). *The Allyn and Bacon guide to peer tutoring* (2nd ed.). New York: Pearson/Longman.

Gillespie, P., & Olson, J. (2002). Tutor training. In B.B. Silk (Ed.), *The writing center resource manual* (2nd ed.) (pp. III.3.1-3.13). Emmitsburg, MD: NWCA Press.

Harvard Writing Project. (2008). Resources for teaching fellows. Retrieved August 21, 2009, from http://isites.harvard.edu/icb/icb.do?keyword=k24101& pageid= icb.page123718.

Hübler. A. (1983). *Understatements and hedges in English*. Amsterdam: John Benjamins.

Kornuta, H. & Germaine, R. Cognitive Level: Bloom's Taxonomy of Educational Objectives. Retrieved August 20, 2009 from http://www.callutheran.edu/ assessment/resources/documents/BloomsTaxonomyCognitiveDomain.pdf.

Robertson, W. (2005). *Writing across borders* (DVD recording). Corvallis: Oregon State University.

Rosenwasser, D. & Stephen, J. (2003). *Writing analytically* (3rd ed.). Boston: Thomson/Wadsworth.

Ryan, L. (2002). *The Bedford guide for writing tutors* (3rd ed.). Boston: Bedford/St. Martin's.

Swales, J.M. & Feak, C.B. (2004). *Academic writing for graduate students: Essential tasks and skills* (2nd ed.). Ann Arbor: University of Michigan Press.

Yaghjian, L.B. (2006). *Writing theology well: A rhetoric for theological and biblical writers*. New York: Continuum.

Chapter 6

Moving from English Literature to General English to English for Theology

Iris Devadason
devadason.iris@gmail.com

Iris Devadason taught English at The United Theological College, Bangalore, affiliated with The Senate of Serampore University, from 1980 to 2006. She has an M.A. in English Literature; her interest in English for Specific Purposes led her to Aston University in Birmingham, U.K. in 1986-87 where she earned an M.Sc. in Applied Linguistics. She has recently submitted a doctoral thesis to the University of Mysore on "Thesis Writing in Theology."

English for Theology may seem like a natural choice for a curriculum for theological students, but it was not always the case. This is the story of how it happened in India, at The Senate of Serampore University.

The Senate of Serampore College in West Bengal was founded in 1818 by missionaries Joshua Marshman, William Carey, and William Ward to educate Protestant Christians in arts and sciences as well as ministry. The Senate today has affiliated colleges all over the Indian subcontinent which focus purely on degrees in theology. Although some secular universities have departments of religion, including Christianity, Serampore remains a unique institution in India for the study of theology alongside other subjects. For high-school graduates, it offers the Bachelor of Theology (B.Th.) degree, for graduates with another bachelor's degree it offers the Bachelor of Divinity (B.D.), and finally, at the highest level it offers a Masters of Theology (M.Th.).

Language policy in multi-lingual India is fraught with the

complexities of colonialism, nationalism, and regionalism. The end result is that English is the medium of instruction at nearly all universities in urban India. Interestingly, theology can be studied in the mother tongue. In the Serampore institutions English is done as a separate course. First-year students do an English course assessed by the local college. Then students take two courses in English called Papers 72 and 73, which are assessed by Senate examiners known as Paper Setters[1] at the end of the second and third years of a four-year program.

However, not all students are equally equipped to study in English. For one thing, students from urban areas are more likely to have attended English-medium secondary schools, while those from rural areas may be weaker in English. The need for English in a student's future may also vary. Students who intend to serve in a congregation where they will need to communicate with churches in other regions of India or the world use English frequently; those in rural congregations have less of a need for this "link language."

It was into this context that I came as an external examiner in the 1980s, later appointed as Convener of the Board of English studies. I found numerous problems. Some colleges insisted that faculty from the Christian Ministry department teach English, as they had some training in teaching methods; some colleges hired part-time and retired staff. Such teachers found this assignment an extra burden and lacked enthusiasm for teaching English. Some colleges did not teach English at all.[2]

Another problem was that English classes were typically literature-oriented. The usual focus on British literature of the 18th and 19th centuries was quite difficult for students, especially from rural backgrounds. Dividing students into those who needed remedial English and those who did not denigrated the vocation of Christian adults and created cultural gaps that were especially sad in a church context. Even strong students could lose confidence in their abilities when faced with unfamiliar and difficult literature. Texts that did not fit the interests and goals of the students also led to lack of motivation. In addition, a literature-based approach led to inappropriate strategies, with students slowly decoding texts instead of being actively involved in reading for

---

1   This system of external examiners, where instructors themselves are not the ones to test students, is designed to ensure integrity.

2   I read one answer from a student who, it turned out, came from an institution with no English teacher. The answer looked like English at first glance, since it was written in the roman script, but the language was actually Hindi!

meaning. Finally, it was simply not helpful for students to spend time on literature, instead of acquiring the theological and academic language that they needed.

A further problem was that the test system itself was problematic, with Paper Setters from all over India not communicating with each other, choosing out-of-print texts, and leaving blanks that were randomly filled in. I was able to pass only about a third of the students whose papers I read. This inspired me to work toward the revision of the English syllabus from a traditional literature-based program toward English for Theological Purposes.

The first step was a recommendation that the study of English literature be replaced by the study of English grammar and skills (reading, writing, speaking, and listening). In the first year, students did five hours of English per week and used general English books that were easily available throughout India. In the second and third years, as they prepared for papers that the Senate would examine, as mentioned above, two books by well-known Indian ELT practitioners were used.[3] In addition, instructors were urged to engage in teaching methodology that would be more positive and encouraging to students, creating an atmosphere congenial to learning. They were to help students help themselves, that is, to learn how to independently read theological prose instead of relying on "bazaar notes." At the same time, to promote flexibility and responsiveness, teachers were told to be creative in meeting the curricular objectives. Finally the evaluation system was revised. Having the first-year evaluation conducted by the colleges instead of the Senate was designed to help students relax and be less afraid of English. The second- and third-year exams were to be done by a qualified committee of examiners, setting papers that would avoid regurgitation of matter learned by heart. The Senate allowed me to conduct workshops for teachers three or four times during this period (as getting teachers from across the nation to meet more often is no easy matter) to encourage them in this new approach.

Another step was that I had by now created some English for Theology materials. I believed that when students read about theology, their background in, familiarity with, and interest in the subject put them automatically on the first rung of the ladder of efficient reading. That was the intent of my book, *Doing Reading in English: A Subject-Specific Textbook of Advanced English for Students of Theology* (1997) with

---

3   N.S. Prabhu and W.W.S. Bhaskar.

texts from theology and accompanying activities designed to take them further up the reading skills ladder.

The book consists of twenty units, each organized around an authentic text on one of seven topics: History of Christianity, Old Testament, New Testament, Religion, Christian Education, Church and Society and Ethics. The topics and texts were chosen in consultation with colleagues in theology. The texts are from classic western works such as Latourette's *A History of Christianity*, Metzger's *The New Testament: Its Background Growth and Content*, and Gustafson's *Theology and Christian Ethics*, as well as from Indian works such as *Baptism in the Malankara Church* and *From Jerusalem to New Delhi*.

The units have various activities: some relate to reading skills, such as skimming, scanning, and study reading, others relate to vocabulary acquisition. Difficult grammar is dealt with by giving students techniques to unpack complex sentences. There are quite a few tasks that help students comprehend difficult discourse as well. For example, they are introduced to the strategy of using a flow chart to follow an author's train of thought, the use of various cohesive devices, typical paragraph patterns, and how to distinguish between a writer's content and comment. Although the emphasis is on reading comprehension, there are some pair and group discussion tasks, and some brief writing assignments. These are to encourage students to share their interpretations of what they have read.

The goal of the book is to enable students to confidently and independently read authentic texts in theology, which they need to do on their own in their second year and beyond. Feedback from B.Th. students in institutions where it has been used has generally been positive. Even students in post-graduate programs, especially some Koreans in the M.Th. program at The United Theological College, where I taught higher-level English, felt the book was very useful. Although the book is now out of print I have sent photocopied versions to colleagues in Southeast Asia and I have heard it is being used in Burma. However, some teachers are intimidated by theology. English for specific purposes is not easy for someone with little background in the subject.

English for Theology is a challenge in terms of teacher training and ongoing materials development, but it is worth it for the benefits it provides students. Teachers who go the extra mile will see their students progress in motivation and language. It is certainly more valuable than the literature-based English program that used to plague students.

Chapter 7
EFL for Theological Purposes in a Small, Changing Program

Urška Sešek[1]
urska.sesek@guest.arnes.si
simona.zabukovec@rkc.si

Urška Sešek holds a Ph.D. in language pedagogy and has been with the English Department of the Faculty of Arts, University of Ljubljana, Slovenia, for twelve years. In addition to TEFL teacher training, language and culture courses, she has taught in various ESP contexts in Slovenia. The current English teacher at the Faculty of Theology in Ljubljana, where the author worked for four years, is Sister Simona Zabukovec, who cooperated in revising this paper.

One of the challenges I faced as the instructor of a course in English for theological purposes in Slovenia was that the situation seemed so idiosyncratic and so unique that it was unlikely anyone else faced my problems or could offer solutions. Yet the factors that make the course special are probably happening in other locations, and there may be many other instructors who are working in relative isolation, but who could profit from sharing ideas with one another.

My purpose in describing the context and challenges of the course

---

1   This chapter was originally written in 2003, and I have since not continued to teach the course described. Therefore, I asked my successor in the post, Sister Simona Zabukovec, the current English instructor at the Faculty of Theology in Ljubljana, to read the manuscript. I thank her wholeheartedly for contributing her perspective and suggesting valuable updates.

in English for theologians at the Faculty of Theology of the University of Ljubljana, Slovenia, is to remind EFL teachers that no matter how isolated we feel, or how grim our situation seems, there are common threads that we can find. There are also common solutions that we can offer each other, as long as the networking takes place.

Slovenia is a country in Central Europe, bordering on Austria, Italy, Hungary and Croatia, with a long history of being part of larger political units, and a period of communism following World War II and ending with independence in 1991. Despite the profound role the Catholic Church has played throughout the country's history, institutional studies of theology in Slovenia have gone through turbulent times. They began in the 16th century with various monastic schools of theology, which were maintained until the Austro-Hungarian authorities dissolved the orders in 1773. For a while, the only way for a young Slovenian male to study theology was at a large Austrian seminary in Graz. In 1811, during the Napoleonic era, the French rulers of Slovenia established the first national university in the capital city of Ljubljana, which included a school of theology. A few decades later the Church founded a separate school of theology in Maribor, the second largest Slovenian town. After World War II this Ljubljana Faculty of Theology was excluded from the University by the communist regime, and only regained its status in 1991.

Today, the Faculty of Theology at the University of Ljubljana, with a branch at the University of Maribor, is the only school of theology in Slovenia. It has approximately 120 students in its five-year course leading to a B.A. degree in theology and double-major courses combining theology with arts courses which students take at other schools within the Universities of Ljubljana and Maribor. Postgraduate courses are also offered.

The curriculum at the Ljubljana Faculty of Theology (as all curricula in Slovenian higher education) consists mostly of required courses, encompassing classical theological subjects such as church history, philosophy, liturgy, Scriptures, law, Latin and Hebrew, but also psychology, educational sciences and foreign languages. Foreign languages such as English, German and Italian have been part of the curriculum for several decades. The purpose of their inclusion was partly to broaden the curriculum and make it more appealing to traditional and new types of students alike, and partly because of a genuine need to equip graduates with a certain proficiency in at least one foreign language in view of the broader societal needs. The school tries to offer courses in several modern foreign languages, but so far English has been by far the most commonly taught. Until 2009 (when educational reforms instituted as part of the European Union's Bologna Process went into effect in Slovenia), all students were required to take a one-year foreign language course. In the future this course will be renamed and will involve fewer hours, but will continue to be the one required language course. The school's official priorities for the course have been to equip students with good reading comprehension and theological English vocabulary to enable them to access and study works of theology written in the English language.

The English Course

What is this single English course like? What can and should it do? What are the pressures its instructor faces? One challenge is the changing student body and the mismatch between official priorities and students' personal goals. Currently in Slovenia, there are not as many traditional seminarians who are preparing for a career in the church. The school is recruiting new types of students and using relatively broad admission criteria. Thus, lay people seeking a university education in the humanities in general, with theology as a mere special interest, and with job goals in publishing, media, or government are enrolling more and more. At least half of the students are women, and there are older adults as well as traditional college-aged students. These students admit that while learning theological English vocabulary is useful, they would prefer to learn general-purpose English. In addition, in terms of language areas to be focused on, their first priority is not reading but speaking.

In terms of proficiency levels which students bring to the course, the school requires all entering students to have passed the national secondary school exit exam, which includes fairly rigorous EFL tests and should in theory ensure that all students are more or less at an upper-intermediate level. In reality, students' English proficiency levels vary from upper elementary to advanced.

Another challenge is administrative, due to class size and enrollment issues. Students can take the course either in their first, second, third or fourth year of studies. The course is repeated each year; as a rule, each student takes it only once, but there is no procedure to control who takes it when, and so students drop and add freely and there may be as few as twenty or as many as forty students in the class. Needless to say, it is usually not possible to make adjustments in terms of schedule, rooms etc. once classes have started.

Motivation varies, but generally does not extend beyond attending class and doing small out-of-class assignments, if they count towards the final grade. Of course, external factors such as course hours, facilities and equipment also influence the syllabus quite significantly sometimes. The school's lecture halls with the typical rows of desks are very counter-productive for a communicative approach to language teaching. Thankfully, equipment such as audio and video players and a data projector have become more readily available to the instructors over the last decade.

I taught the course between 1999 and 2003. Although in the past the course had been taught with a traditional focus on grammar and reading, I instituted a change. First, based on my personal beliefs about language learning and teaching, I leaned towards a communicative approach. Another reason for a more communicative approach was an attempt to meet the expressed needs of the students (while still following the administrative guidelines). I was constrained by the challenges mentioned above, and faced issues which I will discuss later, but nevertheless, I believe the course thus began to serve the diverse students better than it had before.

The course as I designed it featured a topic-based syllabus, covering several topics relevant to the study of Catholic theology (history of the Catholic church, great Catholic personages, the Catholic liturgical year, the Bible, the main symbols and tenets of Christianity), and also some other topics of current relevance for the students, in particular, religion in English speaking countries and around the world, religious tolerance, and employment issues for theologians. In terms of skills, the focus was on reading and listening, with regular in-class speaking activities as a secondary aim, and writing as the least stressed of the four major language skills. There was, as a rule, no explicit teaching of grammar, but vocabulary building was a major concern. Class activities ranged from intensive reading and listening practice (over the past couple of years boosted by the availability of resources such as YouTube) to vocabulary games and information gap speaking activities. The instructor who took the course over from me maintains the same basic framework, with somewhat more stress on grammar as many students need remedial work in this area. A special project that has consistently resulted in keen student involvement has been preparing a full church service in the English language. The students and the instructor prepare by becoming familiar with the parts and the typical common text of the Catholic mass in English. Next, the class learns by heart the responses of the people and some hymns, and individuals prepare the relevant readings and psalms. Finally, a priest who is fluent in English carries out the service in a church near the school with the students as the congregation. In addition to that, the current instructor has introduced visits of English-speaking guests such as missionaries, representatives from the Vatican etc. This contributes to students' motivation and changes their conceptions of English from just another school subject to an important tool of learning and communication in today's world.

Remaining Challenges

One of the main challenges of the course is to provide motivation to ensure active participation of the varied group of students who are obligated to take the course. This is especially difficult in light of the students' widely varying proficiency levels. Inevitably, there are activities in which the advanced students are bored while the weak students are struggling and sometimes even remain passive. Timing is quite difficult to predict as well—students often work at very different speeds, and that means more effort is needed on the part of the teacher to monitor and organize activities as well as to maintain a positive classroom atmosphere.

Internal coherence of the course was another key problem which I could not resolve fully. It seemed quite challenging to determine the most meaningful sequence of topics, especially in terms of regular "recycling," which would at least enable review of vocabulary. It turned out that without some kind of revision built into the course, students, many of whom would prefer to learn general English anyway, retain worryingly little of the specialized vocabulary taught. Having to move on to a new topic in each class session (which is seventy-five minutes long) also resulted in the fact that some topics, issues, and activities were not explored or exploited to their full potential.

While these problems are, I believe, solvable through an increase in teacher investment and expertise, there is another problem related to the character of the course which is beyond the teacher. The assumption behind a specific purpose language class is that the students' subject matter expertise will assist them as they learn the foreign language equivalents of familiar concepts. As mentioned before, many of the students in the course are lay people studying theology. When I began teaching this course I was surprised to find that some students are not even Catholic or religious in any way, and have no background or even interest in theological topics and issues. These students are not familiar with even some basic facts about, for example, the history of Christianity or Catholic liturgy. A quiz on the Bible is thus no longer just a language learning activity, it becomes a subject learning activity, or, to be more precise, it entails learning a subject through a foreign language. While some experts argue that this is the best way to learn a foreign language anyway, I feel that this is detrimental to some extent. Firstly, students are sometimes embarrassed or put off when their lack of subject knowledge or interest in the subject is revealed. Secondly, the chances of a student integrating both new facts and new language items at the same time are in my opinion slimmer than when each task is handled separately.

Last but not least, it is probably obvious from the discussion so far that for a course so specific no prefabricated course book can be used. As the second teacher of this course, I inherited from my predecessor some ideas and a thin collection of loose readings. While this was a start, I felt dissatisfied and tried to locate EFL textbooks for theologians. The two books that I managed to obtain unfortunately turned out to be too demanding for my students both in terms of language level and in terms of content and types of activities. I now believe that the only suitable materials for such a course will be the ones that the teacher prepares him/herself. Such an approach yields a collection of materials whose downside is a certain fragmentation but whose strength is flexibility and freshness. Of course, one adds new materials every year, and the collection grows richer both in terms of quantity and quality as materials and activities are trialled with successive groups of students. Thankfully, the internet is a gold mine of resources for reading as well as listening. Specialized listening materials especially used to be hard to obtain before the spread of easily accessible internet audio and video, but now sermons and many other relevant materials are quite easily located and used in the classroom.

Still, a lot of ingenuity and creativity is required in materials development. One problem facing the materials writer is that while there are numerous English texts around on theological and related topics, they are invariably written for native speaker audiences and therefore have to be shortened, simplified in terms of language or even entirely adapted. Another is that once we have the bare materials, there is the phase of creating activities (pre-, while- and post-reading or listening, quizzes, speaking activities etc.), which can be quite time consuming in view of all the heterogeneity of student needs and contextual constraints.

A separate content and context-related problem for teaching Catholic EFL is that the majority of related materials in the English language come from Protestant traditions (most English-speaking countries being predominantly Protestant). This problem shows up in terminology, especially. Luckily, the internet, again, offers a variety of resources that can come to the instructor's aid, and students can even be assigned mini research projects to compare terminologies. Most importantly, however, they have to be made aware of the fact that language reflects cultural reality.

The existence of this volume is proof that English for theology is a viable branch of ESP. But the situation in Slovenia highlights some issues. Are there enough students of theology learning English to form a critical mass, or is that group, small to begin with, fragmented because of differences in context, denomination, goals, and proficiency?

The EFL course for students of Catholic theology at the University of Ljubljana is indeed the only course of its kind in Slovenia, but I am sure that many of the problems its teacher, students and administrators are facing are familiar to their counterparts in many theological EFL contexts around the world, and I hope that this discussion contributed towards looking for solutions.

Chapter 8

An English Program in a Post-Communist Context

Geraldine Ryan
gryan@oms.org.nz

Geraldine Ryan has been serving with OMS International in Moscow since 1997, where she heads the English program at Moscow Evangelical Christian Seminary. She is also currently working on a Ph.D. in Intercultural Education from Biola University. Her dissertation is titled "Specialized Vocabulary Acquisition Through Texts in the Theology Classroom."

Seven decades of a communist regime left many legacies in Russia. New seminaries, attempting to train future national leaders of the growing evangelical church, have faced two legacies in particular. One is a lack of theological material in Russian and the other is a lack of Russians qualified enough to teach at the graduate level in seminaries. Over the long term, materials are being translated and Russians are pursuing graduate qualifications in theology and related subjects. In the interim, however, seminaries have been using English materials and English-speaking professors to supplement limited Russian resources.

One such example is Moscow Evangelical Christian Seminary (MECS), an interdenominational seminary with a student body from all parts of the former Soviet Union whose common language is Russian. MECS offers two undergraduate degrees (a practically oriented three-year degree and a more academic four-year B.Th. degree) and two masters degrees.

In 1997 the Euro-Asian Accrediting Association (EAAA) was

formed under the auspices of the International Council for Evangelical Theological Education. The EAAA was given responsibility for the accreditation of seminaries in the former Soviet bloc. Included in the standards the EAAA set for accreditation were foreign language requirements. The bachelor-level degrees at MECS have been accredited and the higher degrees are working toward that standard, so the English program has been developed as a response to EAAA requirements.

The EAAA stipulates that unless the major works needed for study are available in Russian, students need to be able to read in English or German. As a result, MECS requires all master's and B.Th. students to study English for three years concurrently with their theological study. The aim is for them to read widely in English for their thesis in their fourth year.

The English Requirement

Initially the English course was run as a one-year intensive. Though ideal for language acquisition, this added an entire year to the students' programs, thus increasing costs for the seminary. (Most Russian students are still unable to pay their full fees and there are no student loans; so money is raised mostly through donations from Western churches and local Christians.) Now, students study English for four hours per week per semester for a total of six semesters, along with three three-week summer intensive courses, for a total of 540 hours.

Because of the narrow aims of the course and the need to take students to an advanced level with only a limited number of hours, the course concentrates on teaching grammar, reading, and vocabulary. There is some speaking, listening, and writing as well, but primarily to support the grammar and reading. Thus, the students have two hours of grammar/listening/speaking and two hours of reading/vocabulary each week for the first four semesters, and each day during the three intensives. In the last two semesters the students work only on reading and vocabulary for all four hours per week.

Although some regular ESL materials are used, much of the course incorporates biblical and theological content. A series of assignments based on Christian reading material has been developed from a high-beginner level through to an advanced level. (For more on these see Chapter 16.)

It requires a lot of effort to acquire a large reading vocabulary in an EFL context when there is little opportunity to hear or use English outside of the classroom. Factors at MECS make the challenge even more difficult. Some of the students enter the seminary with some knowledge of English but there are others, particularly at the B.Th. level, who enter with very little previous English study. The biggest challenge facing the program is to bring such students to an advanced reading level with limited hours of instruction. The seminary curriculum is simply too full to allow for any more hours, however much they might be needed. In addition, because the course runs concurrently with their seminary courses, students are often overwhelmed with other study that is considered more important than English. Therefore they do not always put in the effort, including reading outside the classroom and reviewing vocabulary, which is required to develop the reading skills and the large reading vocabulary they will need.

There are, however, some advantages to studying English concurrently with theology. The students frequently bring a lot of prior knowledge to what they are reading, which sometimes enables them to read authentic texts which would be considered above their actual reading level. In addition, having an understanding of the theological concepts helps with their acquisition of related English vocabulary.

At one level, the English program at MECS is simply a response to accreditation requirements. Like many academic English programs, it struggles with being given enough hours to meet its goals, and this is only exacerbated by the EFL context. But there is a larger view. The theologically-focused reading and vocabulary materials enable future Russian pastors and church leaders to have access to a greater range of material for their study, as well as to interact with the wider Church outside of Russia. In the process, doors are opened for some of them to go on to further graduate-level theological study, thus contributing to the ultimate goal of having Russian seminaries fully staffed by Ph.D.-level Russian professors. These will be the ones who ultimately write theological material in Russian. In this way, the English program is assisting Russians to develop their own resources so that they have less need for English in the long-term.

Chapter 9

Preparing Students to Read Theology in English: Adapting a Standard Curriculum to an Intensive Modular Format

Lois Thorpe
loisthorpe@gmail.com

Lois Thorpe has been teaching at Kyiv Theological Seminary since
2003. She has a Certificate in TESOL from Biola University and is
currently studying for an M.A. in Applied Linguistics at the University
of Birmingham. Lois is a member of SEND International.

Like students in many EFL contexts, those in Kyiv Theological Seminary
have an urgent need to develop reading skills in English. Collaboration
between English and seminary faculty has resulted in a well-designed
program that moves students from beginning reading proficiency to the
ability to read authentic theological materials. Recently, however, the
program has faced a new challenge: accomplishing the same thing with
students who are on campus only for four short intensive sessions each
year. This chapter describes the development of the original curriculum
and its adaptation.

Background

Kyiv Theological Seminary was started in 1995 to give Ukrainian- and
other Russian-speaking students education in theology in their native
language and in their home area. KTS currently offers a four-year B.Th.

and a four-year B.A. (additional summer and winter class session required) in seven specializations (Biblical Studies, Chaplaincy, Christian Education, Church Planting, Pastoral Leadership, Youth Ministry, and World Missions) and an M.A. in Biblical and Theological Studies through Talbot School of Theology.

KTS's faculty and administration is composed of a mix of nationalities. While there are a few resident Ukrainian faculty and several more visiting Ukrainian professors, most of the teaching is done by resident or visiting North Americans. The majority of expatriate teachers reside in Ukraine and teach primarily at KTS. Visiting professors are invited to teach based on their background and expertise in a certain specialization.

In the 1990s few evangelical theological materials were available in Russian, and even fewer in Ukrainian. Although the last several years have brought a surge in translation of Christian books into Russian, there remains a lack of widely available resources, especially academic materials originally written in Russian or Ukrainian. The library at KTS holds 36,000 books; only 38 percent of them are in Russian/Ukrainian, the majority of which are translations from English. Clearly, students need to be able to read in English, both for their studies at KTS and for possible graduate degrees.[1]

The English Courses at KTS

The emphasis in the English courses is on vocabulary and reading. Since published academic reading ESL textbooks covered irrelevant topics and included large sections on writing that we did not need, we had to create many of our own materials. The relatively small size of the faculty at KTS has made it possible for the ESL instructors to collaborate with the theology instructors in the development of these materials. Their input has led to the topics and authentic texts now used in the English classes.

Currently the English curriculum for the residential program consists of three years of English classes with a total of twenty credits: four credits per semester in the first two years and two credits per semester in the third year of study. Students get 300 classroom hours of English. After English classes end, students continue developing in English in their subject matter classes. In the third year of study, those instructors are given the opportunity to assign 10-20 percent of reading in English; in the fourth year, faculty

---

1   A handful of KTS graduates have gone on for graduate degrees in theology at European institutions where the language of instruction is English; several others are doing the Talbot M.A. at KTS where, although instruction is in Russian, approximately half of the assigned reading is in English.

may assign 15-30 percent of reading in English. Figure 1 summarizes the program and the materials used are listed at the end of the chapter. First-year students are typically at a very low level in English. Instruction in the English class is often in Ukrainian/Russian. Lists of common words in English, with Russian glosses and example sentences, are provided for students to learn. Even at this level, however, short authentic materials are given to students (e.g., a short paragraph from BBC online news articles or short passages from the Gospel of John). Out of class, students are asked to work through the vocabulary lists and the readings. In class they summarize the readings in Russian or Ukrainian, so the teacher can see where they might be having difficulties. Class time is also spent on vocabulary activities, reading skills activities, and grammar instruction.

Second-year students are in essence doing the same thing as first-year students but in a more extended way. They are expanding their vocabulary base and adding to their knowledge of biblical and theological words; they are also taught suffixes and prefixes to increase their vocabulary comprehension skills. Their readings are longer and require more analytic responses rather than summaries. Reading exercises teach them to draw conclusions and understand inferences. They begin to learn that text can often not be translated word for word but must be understood in phrases and sometimes from a different worldview perspective.

Third-year students are at a high-intermediate level and the reading texts for the English class include readings that are recommended or required by the theology faculty and that are aligned with the theology courses they are taking, for example, New Testament Survey or Church History. Faculty may recommend readings that complement what is presented in class, or that extend the in-class discussion. The usefulness of the texts is highlighted in their theology class, and the difficulty of the texts is mitigated in the English class as they sort through complex passages with their English instructor.

Even though spoken English is a perceived need by both faculty and students, there is little time to devote to it, with the pressure to take students from beginning to high intermediate reading proficiency in three years. However there are a few ways the tension has been resolved. Although English class is conducted in Russian/Ukrainian at the beginning levels, as students progress, English is spoken in the classroom more and more. Optional assignments are given in second- and third-year classes that include audio recordings and conversational activities. Lastly, students have the opportunity to practice speaking with non-residential English-speaking instructors who visit regularly but have little or no ability in Russian or Ukrainian.

Year	Program	Optional Activities	Interaction with other classes
1st Year	*1st semester:* Basic Vocabulary (400 words); grammar; paragraph to one-page texts (fables, abridged texts, texts about the students themselves). *2nd semester:* Vocabulary (up to 900 words); grammar; one- to three-page texts; graded readers (true stories); reading skills textbook (beginning); modified English Bible studies.		
2nd Year	*3rd semester:* Vocabulary (up to 1,500 words); reading skills textbook (intermediate); simplified Bible commentary reading (2,200 words); graded readers (true stories); four- to five-page texts about topics of interest to students; idioms. *4th semester:* Vocabulary (up to 2,100 words); reading skills textbook (intermediate); two-page texts with audio and activities (podcasts); two-page devotional readings (unabridged); simplified Bible commentary reading (2,200 words).	Podcasts: interviews/ conversations with downloadable text and audio files	
3rd Year	*5th semester:* Academic Word List (180 words); John Piper sermons (text and audio)[1], parallel readings for concurrent classes; chapters/articles on theological topics with emphasis on theological words. *6th semester:* Academic Word List; sermons; parallel readings for concurrent classes; commentaries; short biographies of Christians throughout history.		10-20 percent assigned reading for other classes in English
4th Year			15-30 percent assigned reading for other classes in English

Figure 1: English program for residential students

Year	Pre-Assignments	Program (2-week intensive, 4 hours/day)	Post-Assignments
1st Year	Memorize 150 vocabulary words; read overview of grammar and note the differences between Russian/Ukrainian and English	*Summer session*: Basic vocabulary (350 words); grammar; read paragraph to one-page texts (fables, abridged texts, texts about the students themselves)	Read one-page texts, write a summary of the texts, optional podcasts (reading and audio)
2nd Year	*Winter session:* Review vocabulary, memorize 150 new words, read one graded reader, Bible study activities to introduce theological vocabulary	*Winter session:* Vocabulary (up to 900 words); grammar; one- to three-page texts; graded readers (true stories); reading skills textbook (beginning); modified English Bible studies	*Winter session:* Reading (50 pages); vocabulary review exercises; optional podcast activities
	Summer session: Review vocabulary, memorize 150 new words; read one graded reader	*Summer session:* Vocabulary (up to 1,500 words); reading skills textbook (intermediate); simplified Bible commentary reading (2,200 words); graded readers (true stories); four- to five-page texts about topics of interest to students; introduce idioms	*Summer session:* Reading (graded commentary); vocabulary review exercises; optional podcast activities
3rd Year	Review vocabulary; memorize 150 new words; read one graded reader, read first two chapters in graded study/commentary that students will do during session	*Winter session*: Vocabulary (up to 2,100 words); reading skills textbook (intermediate); two-page texts with audio and activities (podcasts); two-page devotional readings (unabridged); simplified Bible commentary reading (2,200 words)	Commentary reading and response; optional podcast activities
4th Year			

Figure 2: English program for modular students

Residential vs. Modular Instruction

From the time the doors of KTS opened, there have been parallel programs for residential ("full-time") and modular ("part-time") students, a system of study that is widely accepted in Ukraine. At KTS, the modular programs traditionally consist of two-week sessions four times a year. Students are thus able to continue in their ministries, at their work and with their families, rather than being extracted from their homes and relocating to the relatively expensive city of Kyiv in order to study full-time. As an institution, KTS wants to allow students to continue in the ministries they are already involved in, while providing them with the practical, theological education they need to grow in these ministries.

The administration at KTS has always attempted to keep the curriculum of modular and residential programs as similar as possible so that students are receiving equivalent degrees. In 2008, the curriculum was revised to offer two additional two-week sessions to modular students who desire to earn B.A. degrees, equivalent to Western standards, rather than the B.Th., which was their only previous option. This would facilitate students' applications to master's level programs at either secular or theological schools with Western accreditation. The curriculum revision brought the total number of modules to six sessions per year. It also added the option of English to modular students for the first time.

As noted above, the residential students have 300 hours of English spread over their first three years, with English reading assigned in both third- and fourth-year theology courses. The modular program, on the other hand, allows for just twelve units or 160 classroom hours. In addition, these hours are distributed differently, with students studying English intensively for two weeks at a time, twice in their first year and twice in their second year. Figure 2 summarizes the new modular program.

Adapting the Existing English Curriculum to a Modular Format

Revising the curriculum to fit into this modular program has presented a fair number of challenges. The first challenge is the drastic reduction in the number of hours allotted to English. How much can be accomplished in only four 40-hour sessions? The response to this challenge for all modular classes has been to design pre- and post-assignments. Students must understand that much of their study will be independent. Classroom time is used to clarify questions, and to give them the tools they need to improve their English, which they have to continue to do on their own.

A related challenge of the modular system is that there is a six-month gap between sessions, making it easy for students to forget what they have learned or lose momentum. The schedule of assignments is designed to lessen this gap. Pre-assignments are given six weeks in advance; post-assignments are due four weeks after the module has ended. Since students are engaged with English before and after their on-campus session, the gap has been reduced to only four months. In addition, although students do not have English class at the time, they are on campus two other times during the semester. Informal meetings between students and English staff keep them engaged during these times. Additional materials for review at home are being developed, including recordings of the vocabulary and reading texts for students to listen to.

The third challenge is that English is optional for modular students. This means that the theology faculty cannot assign reading in English to third- and fourth-year modular students, as they can in the residential program. As only about one-third of the modular students are studying English, this essentially removes both a motivator to study English and an opportunity to continue improving in English in their other seminary classes. Nevertheless, the faculty can include suggested or additional reading in English in their syllabi. Students already ask teachers for additional resources in some areas, but often the answer is that there is not much available unless students read English. The hope is that the quest for good theological content will keep students eager to learn English.

Finally, the cohort system of keeping students together in the same courses for their four-year period of study has not been as strictly followed in modular classes. A modular English class might thus have students from each year of study and, therefore, varying background knowledge from theology courses.

Two Weeks in the Classroom

What do the intensive English classes look like in the modular program? Students are on campus for two weeks, spending four hours a day in English class, and four hours in another subject class. This limits how much homework or review they can be expected to do between classes. The beginners arrive having done a basic overview of grammar differences between English and Russian/Ukrainian and having memorized 150 vocabulary items. In-class time is spent on 350 more vocabulary words, grammar, and the reading of short texts.[2] Every day students are expected to learn another thirty words, which are then reviewed and tested. With

---

2   One-paragraph texts were taken from Folse, *Beginning Reading Practices*; longer texts can be found in Mikulecky & Jeffries, *Basic Reading Power*. See ESL Texts Used in this Program for bibliographic information.

an emphasis still on reading, each evening students are assigned to read through short texts with in-class review for a comprehension check. At the end of their two weeks students are able to read and understand short stories and are ready for the post-assignment, to read and summarize eight to ten one-page texts, with the summaries written in Russian. They are also given optional reading/listening activities for the few months between sessions. The progress they have made motivates them to persevere.

Conclusion

As this is a new program, I cannot draw definite conclusions about its potential for success. My initial experience with an intensive for the modular students indicates that they made progress comparable to students in the residential program. The beginning students were surprised at how quickly they were able to apply their knowledge and begin to comprehend the texts they had to read.

However, although students may be able to reach intermediate reading proficiency, we have yet to see the effect of them missing the third-year piece in our residential program. This is the year in which students are guided through parallel assignments in both their theology and English classes. Nevertheless, the hope is that if students are self-motivated and can see their progress, they will gain and use the tools they need to take on the English language at a more academic or theological level.

ESL Texts Used in this Program
(Sorted by Level)

English 1

Beaumont, D. (1993/2001). *Heinemann ELT elementary English grammar*. Russian Version. Kiev: Metodika.

Folse, K. (1996). *Beginning reading practices*. Ann Arbor: University of Michigan Press.

Kachalova, K.N. and Izrailevich, E.E. (1997). *Praktickiskaya grammatika Angliskovo yazika* (Practical English grammar). Volumes 1 and 2. Kiev: Metodika.

Mikulecky, B. and Jeffries, L. (2004). *Basic reading power* (2nd ed.). New York: Longman.

English 2

Border, R. (2003). *The piano*. Oxford: Oxford University Press. (Graded Reader: Level 2)

Eby, J. W. and Troutman, P. (1988). *Gospel of John: Who is Jesus?* Kansas City: Beacon Hill Press.

Vicary, T. (2000). *The coldest place on earth*. Oxford: Oxford University Press. (Graded Reader: Level 1).

Vicary, T. (2000). *The elephant man*. Oxford: Oxford University Press. (Graded Reader: Level 1).

www.podcastsinenglish.com.

www.britishcouncil.org/learnenglish-podcasts.

English 3

Beaumont, D. and Granger, C. (1989/2000). *Heinemann ELT English grammar*. Russian Version. Kiev: Metodika.

Dickens, C. (2000) *A Christmas carol*. Oxford: Oxford University Press. (Graded Reader: Level 3).

Folse, K. (2004). *Intermediate reading practices*. (3rd ed.). Ann Arbor: University of Michigan Press.

Kachalova, K.N. and Izrailevich, E.E. (1997). *Praktickiskaya grammatika Angliskovo yazika (Practical English grammar)*. Volumes 1 and 2. Kiev: Metodika.

www.britishcouncil.org/learnenglish-podcasts.

www.easyenglish.info/bible-commentary.

www.easyenglish.info/bible-study.

www.podcastsinenglish.com.

www.voanews.com/specialenglish/index.cfm.

English 4

Dumas, A. (2000) *The count of monte cristo*. London: Penguin Longman. (Graded Reader: Level 3).

Folse, K. (2004). *Intermediate reading practices*. (3rd ed.). Ann Arbor: University of Michigan Press.

Mikulecky, B. and Jeffries, L. (2004) *Reading power*. (3rd ed.). Massachusetts: Addison-Wesley Publishing Company.

www.britishcouncil.org/learnenglish-podcasts.

www.easyenglish.info/bible-commentary.

www.easyenglish.info/bible-study.

www.podcastsinenglish.com.

www.voanews.com/specialenglish/index.cfm.

English 5 and 6

Benge, J. and Benge, G. (various dates). *Christian heroes: Then & now series*. Seattle: YWAM Publishing. (34 volumes).

Dodd, D. (2003). *Dictionary of theological terms in simplified English*. Wheaton: EMIS.

Foster, R. and Griffin, E. (2000). *Spiritual classics*. San Francisco: Harper.

Foster, R. and Smith, J.B. (1990). *Devotional classics*. San Francisco: Harper.

Pierson, C. (2003). *Dictionary of theological terms in simplified English: Student workbook*. Wheaton: EMIS.

Stevenson, R.L. (2003). *Treasure island*. Oxford: Oxford University Press (Graded Reader: Level 4).

www.desiringgod.org/ResourceLibrary/.

Chapter 10
English for Academic and Communicative Purposes in an International Seminary

Nancy K. Alvarez
pnalvarez@yahoo.com

Nancy Alvarez has been a missionary in Japan and the Philippines since 1984. She has served with SEND, CBInternational, and Campus Crusade for Christ. She has an M.A. in Missions/Intercultural Studies and a Certificate in TESL from Wheaton Graduate School. She currently lives in Orlando, Florida and writes for the JESUS Film Project, a ministry of Campus Crusade for Christ. She taught TESL at IGSL from 1997 to 2006.

The International Graduate School of Leadership (IGSL) in Manila, Philippines provides seminary and missions training for Asians. Christian leaders from many Asian nations are eager for quality education, yet need to overcome barriers such as the lack of a seminary in their home country, high costs if they should study in a western nation, or the temptation to stay in a more comfortable western nation. IGSL-Asia, (formerly International School of Theology-Asia), an interdenominational and evangelical school, is a Campus Crusade for Christ-affiliated seminary which provides such an opportunity not only for Filipinos, but also for students from places such as Bangladesh, Myanmar, Sri Lanka, India, Nepal, Indonesia, Korea, and Vietnam. IGSL offers the following degrees: Master of Divinity, Master of Biblical Studies, Master of Christian Leadership, Master of Theology and Doctor of Ministry. Enrollment averages 150-200 students per year.

A key feature of IGSL is that tuition is kept affordable, even for those from very poor nations, by having faculty members, both Western and Asian, raise their own support as missionaries. Besides affordability, IGSL's appeal is that students trained in Asia are uniquely prepared to lead the churches of Asia and reach other Asians with the gospel of Jesus Christ. At the same time, since the Philippines is an officially Christian country, it offers a special benefit, especially to students from nations closed to Christian witness. Students are able to experience personal evangelism and church planting strategies without fear of reprisal, thus gaining skills from experience as well as knowledge from classrooms.

Although there are many benefits and fewer barriers when these leaders study in the Philippines, compared to studying in a western country, there is still one big challenge. Since the seminary is international, instruction is in English. Even when students come with a fairly high level of English, there is still more to learn. Students have four main English learning needs: studying graduate-level theological material, engaging in the experiential co-curriculum of IGSL, getting around in daily life in the Philippines, and (possibly in the future) engaging in ongoing international communication since they are among the top Christian leaders of their nations.

English Intensive Training

To meet these needs, IGSL has an English Intensive Training (EIT) program. Each non-native English speaking applicant to the seminary must take an English Proficiency Test (EPT) and pass with a score of 80 percent or higher to be fully accepted into a degree program. This test is sent to students as part of the application process; it is to be administered by a trusted proctor. Those who score between 50-79 percent are required to enroll in the EIT program. Those who score lower than 50 percent are encouraged to improve their English at home first, both because of our limited teaching staff, and because it is usually not cost-effective for someone to move to the Philippines only to spend more than a year just on preparatory English study.

The EPT was created by IGSL faculty members and gauges applicants' abilities not only in grammar, reading, listening, and writing, but also their understanding of theological themes and their ability to describe Christian experiences. It includes a section in which students read paragraphs from an apologetics book and answer comprehension questions, a writing section in which they describe their salvation testimony, and a recording of a portion of a seminary lecture which they listen to in order to answer questions.

There are several versions of the EPT so that when students need to repeat the exam they will not pass merely because they memorized the questions. Students placed in EIT take classes for six months to one year, studying four to five days a week in two hour sessions. The classes prepare students both to pass the EPT and also to be successful in their seminary tasks. This means that they learn to read complex theological material, write research papers, understand their professors' lectures and their classmates' comments, and participate in class discussions. In addition, there is a focus on communicative English related to the co-curriculum which will be described later. Classes are small. Students are given individual attention, remedial classes and tutoring when needed. This enables some students to make dramatic progress even in a few months.

Some published communicative-style ESL textbooks are used, but more often in-house materials created by EIT staff are used. These enable the teachers to teach grammar, reading, writing, listening, and speaking through topics of importance and interest to the students. Thus, students may read about predestination, talk about their testimony, listen to each other share about a missions experience, or write about grief counseling. Teachers are encouraged to interact with their students and listen to their stories so that the materials created are relevant. Lunch at the school canteen or dinner in a faculty member's home are occasions when the faculty hear their students' stories—such as how an Indonesian Bible translator escaped from a serious tribal conflict, or how a Bangladeshi student was disinherited by his Muslim religious leader father.

English in the Co-curriculum

As mentioned, IGSL has an experiential co-curriculum which means that students have more communicative demands placed on them than may be true in other seminaries. For example, twice a year all students, staff and faculty travel to outlying areas to assist churches in ministries such as evangelism and lay training. Students need the English skills to give their testimony, engage in evangelism, and teach a variety of seminars. In addition, each student is also enrolled in what is called an "Iron Sharpening Group." Five to seven students meet with a faculty member weekly for character development, skills training, as well as care and nurturing. With groups consisting, for example, of students from India, Indonesia, Thailand, and the Philippines, along with an American faculty member, a high level of conversational ability is required. Finally, all students are required to complete at least one internship during their stay. They work as part of a team to further develop their skills in evangelism, discipleship and church planting. Again, fluent English is a must.

IGSL expects the wives of the male students to participate in their husband's ministry and develop their own ministry skills. To this end, there is a two-year certificate program called Partners in Ministry (PIM). The EIT program includes classes for the non-native English speaking women so that they can get the most out of the PIM program. Besides a typical ESL curriculum, their classes include the English needed to share their personal testimony, distribute gospel tracts, and engage in other ministry. The classes also provide the opportunity to get to know others in a non-threatening environment. Women share prayer requests and pray for each other too.

Another program of IGSL is a one-year certificate in Teaching English as a Second Language (TESL). This program produces most of our EIT teachers, and TESL trainees are available for tutoring seminary students. When TESL trainees do their practice teaching in the EIT classes, the students have the benefit of hearing new voices in English.

Issues

Although we are pleased with the EIT program and confident of its strategic value in helping these Asian leaders get the training they need, there are on-going issues that need to be dealt with. One is the necessary standard of English that students need to reach before enrolling in seminary classes. IGSL leadership wants to maintain high standards and save the seminary faculty from struggles such as reading an incomprehensible paper, yet there are other occasions when they want to make exceptions. There may be a student from a "closed" country, for example, for whom studies at IGSL would be very strategic, yet who has little opportunity to study more English at home. Should this student be admitted without the usual EPT score?

There have been cases where a student with only a two-year leave from his home country or workplace has been granted provisional acceptance into IGSL pending passage of the EPT after an intensive pre-course program. When it turns out that was not enough time and the student needs a full year of English before taking their regular IGSL classes, they do not have time to finish their degree. Furthermore, some students have technically passed the EPT, yet still need remedial help in some areas. This is related to another issue: on-going improvement of the EPT so that it is an instrument with more validity and reliability for our purposes.

We face the practical problems of most programs, such as scheduling English classes so that they do not conflict with seminary classes, or teaching several proficiency levels in one class due to limited teaching staff. A final challenge is curriculum development, so our materials are maximally useful for these students.

IGSL exemplifies the use of English in the world today. No longer the exclusive domain of native speakers, English is a bridge language for people all over the world to communicate with each other. IGSL's English language program, therefore, needs to prepare students not only for the academic challenges of studying theology in English, but also for the communicative challenges of going about daily life in English and doing ministry in English. Part of our success is due to a caring environment, where faculty, staff, and students are family to each other. It is also due to the use of relevant materials that grow out of the students' own experiences and needs.

Chapter 11
A Diverse EFL Program for Both Seminary and Community Students

Jan E. Dormer
jan.dormer@gmail.com

Jan Edwards Dormer, Ed.D. has worked in English language
development and seminary education in Brazil and Indonesia since
1995. She currently directs a Master of Education program in
Indonesia, teaches at Anderson University in Indiana, and is involved in
leadership in TESOL, Inc.

Over the past ten years I have worked with two seminaries founded by
OMS International: one in Brazil and one in Indonesia. Both are Protestant theological training schools for pastors and other ministry workers.
Both schools have been operating for some time—roughly sixty and forty
years respectively, but each began to face new realities around the turn of
the century. These new realities, ushered in by the global economy, were a
need for more effective English instruction, and a need for increased income.
An English program which sought to meet these needs was developed
first in Brazil, and then later used also in Indonesia.

In 2000, I was asked to begin an English program within the seminary
in Brazil. I envisioned a program which would serve both the seminary
students and the general public. The seminarians would receive more
effective English instruction, and fees from students outside the seminary
would help meet the financial needs of the seminary. Such a program
would be diverse both in clientele and in content. It would have to provide
the content-specific instruction needed in seminary English classes, while

at the same time appealing to the public. I also wanted it to be a ministry to the public. I wanted all who came to our program, whether Christians or not, to be blessed and edified through our English classes.

Was such a school possible? I believed that it was, and thus what is now called "English for Life" was born, with the motto, "Where English comes to life, enhances life, and promotes true Life."

Program Development

Three foundational requirements were established as the program began. First, in order to meet the English language needs of seminary students, the program had to include not only a solid foundation in general English, but also introduce Biblical and church language. Second, in order to provide income for the seminary, the program would need to appeal to the general public by offering something unique—something that the dozens of other English schools in the city were not offering. Finally, it was important to me that this program also provide an opportunity for the seminary students and Christian teachers to engage in ministry. This meant that it should be openly identified as a Christian language school, and that during the class sessions there should be occasions for constructive dialogue about values, faith, and Christianity.

A very flexible program was needed to meet these diverse requirements, and our three-person start-up staff began envisioning how the program might work. I began writing a task-based curriculum—a curriculum which focuses on what students can actually *do* with English, as opposed to what they might *know* about English. Teachers contributed ideas about out-of-class learning opportunities which we could provide. Student surveys were conducted. Over the next couple of years, the "English for Life" program emerged, with the following key features:

(1) "Core classes" based on a task-based syllabus
(2) A wide variety of electives, called "modules"
(3) One-on-one speaking and writing opportunities
(4) Student control over many aspects of their study
(5) Collections of authentic materials for each level, from which teachers select what is most appropriate for each student group

Program Description

The English for Life program is a collection of learning opportunities (see Table 1) within a strong and supportive language learning community.[1] With varied opportunities and choices, students take part in designing their own program of study, meeting their own learning goals and capitalizing on their own strengths and interests. Students study a minimum of six hours weekly: four hours in the Core Class, and at least two hours (or more, if desired) selected from among the other learning opportunities.

Class/Opportunity	Content	Suggested hours per week
Core Class (levels 1-5)	• The *English for Life* curriculum (the majority of the class time should be spent covering this curriculum) • Supplementary grammar (we suggest *Basic Grammar in Use* by Raymond Murphy) • Bible verses (if appropriate)	4
Modules	• High interest topics such as "American Cooking" or "Listening to Music" • These provide an opportunity to *use* English in non-classroom settings	1 per module (Students may be involved in several modules)
Group learning	• A class in which students of all levels learn together through singing, games, and other fun activities. • Multi-level teaching techniques are used, and students are encouraged to help and support one another.	1
Self-directed learning	• An opportunity for students to engage in individualized study, with teachers and materials available to help them.	1

---

1 Teachers also viewed themselves as language learners. Those who were native English speakers were struggling to learn the local language, and Brazilian or Indonesian teachers viewed themselves as "lifelong learners of English." These attitudes resulted in camaraderie with students, and a strong learning community at the school.

Class/Opportunity	Content	Suggested hours per week
Conversation time (one-on-one)	• An opportunity for students to informally engage in conversation with a competent English speaker.	15-20 min.
Email buddies	• An opportunity for students to have a "pen pal" overseas who will write to them in English (a good opportunity for volunteers in churches or elsewhere)	No specific time
Church services or other events in English	• These opportunities can significantly increase students' motivation in language learning, and their exposure to English.	Monthly

Table 1: Learning Opportunities

Core Classes are the backbone of this program. These are leveled classes in which students engage in communicative language learning. Some grammar instruction is included in the core classes, though it does not feature prominently in the program. (Students who want more grammar study can enroll in a module on grammar.) The Core Classes are divided into five levels, ranging from beginning to high-intermediate. Each level focuses on a central theme, and includes eight units on topics related to the theme (see Table 2).

Level	Theme	Sample Content
1	Introduction to English	letters, numbers, colors, food, body, clothing, school, personal information
2	Home and Family	introductions, descriptions, jobs, home life, family, house, schedules and habits
3	Community	the neighborhood, stores, services, directions, professions
4	The World	culture, customs, holidays, geography, countries
5	Personal Development	relationships, traditions, beliefs, worldview, problems and solutions, change, the future

Table 2: Theme and content for the five levels

The task-based syllabus that is utilized in the Core Classes is presented to students at the beginning of each level as their "Ability Checklist" (see sample in Appendix). This checklist guides the teaching and learning process in the Core Classes. Reading, writing, speaking and listening tasks are the focus, with grammar instruction provided as needed to enable the tasks. Materials are usually authentic (that is, not originally designed for language study), student-produced, or teacher-made.

While students are placed in a Core Class on the basis of a placement test, students can generally choose which modules they want to take. A few modules are academic in nature, such as "grammar" and "pronunciation," but most focus on skills, pastimes or English for specific purposes. Sometimes the modules simply provide an opportunity to *use* English. Module leaders are often visiting volunteers who speak little of the local language, so learners are more motivated to use English to communicate. Modules that everyone can enjoy might include travel, current events, listening to music, movies, cooking, crafts, woodworking, and aerobics. However, the module system is also one of the ways in which this program provides the Christian content needed by the seminarians. Modules on topics such as worship leading, missions and Bible study can both further ministerial skills and equip students with subject-specific English vocabulary.

All students beyond the introductory level have the opportunity for individual weekly conversation times with a native speaker, called "One on One." These times are often spent doing a task from the Ability Checklist. For example, a student working on the task "I can *talk* about my abilities and talents in relation to jobs and activities," taken from the Ability Checklist excerpt shown in the Appendix, might talk with his conversation partner about the abilities and talents that he uses in his job or ministry. His teacher might have helped him prepare for this session by teaching vocabulary related to this topic, and even conducting a pair activity so he could practice the conversation with a partner in class.

Students in the upper levels may also sign up to be paired with "Email Buddies." These are native speaking volunteers, largely from churches in North America, who correspond with students by email. This gives students opportunities to achieve some of the writing goals on their Ability Checklists, while at the same time forging friendships and serving the ministry goals of the program.

The modules, conversation times and email opportunities all contribute to a program that is fundamentally student-centered in that they provide students with a great deal of control over the content of their studies. But the program is student-centered in another key aspect as well: students themselves decide when they are ready to move from one level to the next. Usually, a student can complete a level in one semester, but many busy students need additional time. Since teachers draw materials from a resource file rather than a textbook, students can go through the same level twice, using different materials. Repeat students also experience the same level differently the second time around because of the use of student-created materials. When teachers use students' writing as the basis for a reading assignment, for example, the material will be new each semester, and will continually cater to the needs and interests of the current student group.

There is no testing in this program. Evaluation occurs twice during the semester, and consists of student conferences with the teacher. At the conference, the student presents a portfolio of work completed to date, evidence of attendance and homework completion, and, most importantly, his Ability Checklist, with the tasks that he can successfully accomplish in English checked. During the midterm evaluation, the teacher and student will decide together what changes, if any, must be made in order to improve the students' language acquisition. The conference may result in a commitment to change something, either on the part of the student or on the part of the teacher. If sufficient progress is not being made in the writing tasks, for example, the student may commit to writing to his email buddy once a week. Or the teacher may need to make a commitment, such as working with the student to complete an extra writing assignment each week. At the final evaluation conference of the semester, student and teacher come to a consensus about the student's placement in the coming semester. They will decide together whether the student should move on or stay in the same level.

The Program in Practice

To see how the English for Life program meets the needs of both seminary students and those from the community, we will now look at how one Level 5 class might work for two very different students in Brazil.[2] (See the Appendix for the Ability Checklist for Level 5.) Dennis is a seminary student. He represents about 1/3 of the students in the class

---

2   Dennis and Rosa are fictitious, but are composites of real students who have studied at English for Life.

who are seminarians, pastors, or missionaries, and are upgrading their English skills for ministry purposes. Rosa is a non-Christian economics professor at a local university. Rosa is an agnostic, and would not normally attend a Christian English program. However, she chose English for Life because of its reputation for preparing students to interact with native speakers—a skill that she needs when she attends international conferences and assists visiting professors at her university. Her initial conversation with the teacher puts her at ease and makes her feel as though the teacher will accept and respect her, so she is prepared to give it a try. She has been warned that she will need to memorize a Bible verse during each unit, but a look at the list of verses assures her that these are passages generally known to well-educated individuals (she knows some of them in Portuguese because of her Catholic upbringing), and she wouldn't mind knowing them in English.

The first unit in Level 5 is entitled "Personality/Spiritual Gifts." Students are given the option of taking a personality test or a spiritual gifts inventory. Dennis chooses the latter. He has never done this before and finds he is challenged to consider his strengths and weaknesses in ministry. Rosa asks the teacher to explain "spiritual gifts" because she has never heard this expression before. In response to Rosa's question, the teacher explains that spiritual gifts are a biblical description of how different people have different abilities. Rosa opts to take the personality test. In discussion activities afterwards, Rosa finds that the other students are interested in hearing about her personality and she finds herself intrigued by the results of their spiritual gifts inventories as well.

In the second unit, "Life Story/Testimony," Rosa is asked to tell the class about her life. The seminary students, including Dennis, are doing what seems to her to be the same thing, but calling it a "testimony." Dennis's classmates are touched by his testimony and ask him many questions, especially about why he is becoming a pastor.

The whole class reads two texts in the next unit on "Life Adventures/ Mission Trips." One reading is about an archeological dig in the Middle East, and one is about a mission trip to Angola. Rosa is asked to choose one of the readings to summarize in a paragraph, and she chooses the archeological dig, even though she found the mission trip reading interesting as well. Dennis is given a different follow-up activity because his teacher thinks it will be interesting for him: he reads some excerpts from English resources in the library about Angola and the work of the church there.

The next unit is "Change." Dennis knows this is an important topic in Christian ministry. Included among the materials in the unit is a dialogue about change in the church. This proves so thought-provoking to Dennis that he talks about the topic with his own pastor the next weekend. During this unit the teacher asks Rosa whether she deals with a lot of change in her job, and Rosa immediately and wearily answers, "Constantly!" The teacher views this as an open door for the other students to hear more about Rosa's reality, and follows up with questions. Rosa tells the class that due to a recent prolonged university strike, class schedules and curricula have been altered, and professors are experiencing a lot of stress. The class listens sympathetically and Rosa appears to have appreciated the opportunity to share.

In the unit about "Problems and Solutions," Rosa is asked to choose a problem that is typical in her work. She ends up writing and speaking about unmotivated college students, a topic which interests her classmates as well. The teacher encourages Dennis to focus on a problem in the church, for example, the lack of Sunday school teachers. As Dennis writes and speaks about problems and solutions, he even interviews a local missionary (in English) to get additional perspectives.

"Social/Christian Responsibility" is the next unit, and the entire class listens to a recording of a news program about an outbreak of disease due to poor sanitation in a slum area in Malaysia. All students are asked to write about possible causes and possible solutions. Rosa believes that the Malaysian government should do more to solve this kind of problem. In small groups, students discuss their ideas about solutions and Rosa is surprised that some students don't share her opinion. She enjoys the ensuing debate and feels that the teacher and other students respect the differing points of view expressed. Dennis has appreciated the chance to think about how the church might approach such problems.

The next unit, "Ethical Dilemmas" is one that Rosa is looking forward to, since she frequently considers ethical questions when teaching economics. The teacher gives each student an ethical question and asks them to present a solution to the class. Rosa's is about taxation and large business corporations. Dennis's is about financial management in Christian organizations.

The semester ends with a unit on "Future Plans." Dennis is encouraged by the teacher to think and write about God's will for his future ministry. Rosa is given an opportunity to speak to the class about her dream of going abroad to pursue a doctorate in economics. Her teacher and classmates encourage her, and one even says he'll pray for her. Rosa is not accustomed to hearing that phrase, but it makes her feel valued.

We have seen here how the Core Class topics are tailored for individual students. Student needs are also met through the Modules. Rosa is intent on the academic study of English, and opts to take modules on both Grammar and Pronunciation. When she has one-on-one conversation time with a missionary teacher at the school, they often discuss aspects of teaching, such as how to increase student motivation. Rosa's e-mail buddy is a retired financial analyst. Rosa has only corresponded a couple of times with him, but has already learned some new English vocabulary related to her profession.

As for Dennis, he has chosen four modules: English Bible study, Worship leading, Choir, and Pronunciation. In the first three, especially, he is learning Christian terminology in English. Dennis's one-on-one time with a missionary gives him more opportunities to talk about ministry in English. He considers his conversation time to be mentorship, not just an English class activity, and has a similar relationship with his email buddy, who is a deacon in a church in Canada. For Dennis, these mentoring relationships are the best part of the English for Life program.

Exporting the Program

In 2004 my family and I had to leave Brazil due to visa problems, and were sent by our organization to Indonesia. This provided a perfect opportunity to see if the English for Life program could also be successful in another seminary in a very different culture. It is important for any program to adapt to local contextual realities, and so a number of changes were made. The memorization of Bible verses was optional for those in the program who were not seminary students—an important change if we wished to attract students from the community, who would likely be Muslims. Because Indonesians favor community over individualization, conversation times became small group encounters rather than intimidating one-on-one sessions. Also because of the strong emphasis on community, we began "Group Learning" sessions (see Table 1), which proved to be very effective in Indonesia.

A key to the success of any program in a new context is to adapt to local realities, but sometimes a new idea can work even though it is initially foreign to students. Our evaluation system was just such an idea in Indonesia. For students accustomed to high-stakes multiple choice testing, our system of evaluating through ongoing checklists and periodic conferences was at first met with disbelief. However, I felt that students would benefit by taking more control over their own learning and evaluation, and I didn't back down. My persistence paid off. After the first semester, students became more relaxed and involved in their English learning, and grew to appreciate our more individualized and authentic evaluation system. Sometimes it is difficult to know when to introduce new ideas and when to adapt to more traditional ways. Sensitivity, respect, cultural understanding and dialogue with local teachers and students are crucial when adapting a program such as English for Life to a new context.

Conclusion

Language is usually not acquired through a single activity, but rather through a multitude of diverse activities. When immigrants to English-speaking countries learn the language, they do so by going to classes in English, going shopping in English, watching T.V. in English, and talking to their neighbors in English. These diverse activities combine to "individualize" their language learning tasks, and provide multiple sources of language input. Such diversity is hard to duplicate in EFL settings, where English is often only used in the English class. But the English for Life program tries to do just that with its multiple learning opportunities. At the same time, it is designed to allow for engagement in ministry on a number of levels. Seminarians are prepared for ministry, and non-believers see Christianity lived out on a daily basis in the lives of Christian students and staff. Topics of discussion support the development of values and promote growth and learning for all. A frequently heard comment from students in all categories is, "This is more than an English school; it is a caring family. My life has improved because I came here." By opening its doors to the public, a seminary can put into action Christ's words in Matthew 5:16: "Let your light shine before men, that they may see your good deeds and praise your Father in heaven."

Appendix
Ability Checklist, Level 5
Personal Development

Name: _____ Date: _____

Check each task when you can do it with a proficient speaker and with at least 70 percent accuracy.

1. Personality / Spiritual Gifts
   - ❑ I can *take* a personality test or spiritual gifts inventory.
   - ❑ I can *talk* about my abilities and talents in relation to jobs and activities.
   - ❑ I can *describe* my personality to a friend, and *answer* questions.
   - ❑ I can *write* a one-page summary of my personality, abilities and talents.
   - ❑ I can *read* about someone's personality, and *ask* follow-up questions.
   - ❑ Vocabulary: I know thirty character quality adjectives.

2. Life Story / Testimony
   - ❑ I can *write* my personal testimony, suitable for a publishing.
   - ❑ I can *give* my personal testimony.
   - ❑ I can *read* a short (one-two pages) biography or testimony, and *answer* questions.
   - ❑ I can *ask* questions and find out about a person's past.
   - ❑ I can *answer* someone's questions, telling about my past.
   - ❑ Vocabulary: I know the words of life stages.

3. Life Adventures / Mission Trips
   - ❑ I can *read* about an adventure, and *answer* questions.
   - ❑ I can *interview* someone about an adventure.
   - ❑ I can *write* a summary of an interview.
   - ❑ I can *plan* a missions (or adventure) trip, doing research and taking notes.
   - ❑ I can *present a talk* on a missions (or adventure) trip, using visuals.
   - ❑ Vocabulary: I know nouns and adjectives for countries and people.

4. Change
   - ❑ I can *read* about a changed life, and *understand* the main idea.
   - ❑ I can *tell* about someone who had a significant life change.
   - ❑ I can *discuss* change, and *understand* why change is difficult.
   - ❑ I can *do research* about a habit that many people want to change.
   - ❑ I can *give a talk* about how to achieve a desired change.
   - ❑ Vocabulary: I know expressions for habits.
   - ❑ Vocabulary: I can describe life change in writing and speaking.

5. Problems and Solutions
   - ❏ I can *read* about a problem, and *discuss* it, giving suggestions.
   - ❏ I can *write* a response to a problem, giving advice.
   - ❏ I can *write* about a problem, asking for advice.
   - ❏ I can *apply* biblical principles to a current problem.
   - ❏ I can *pray* about a problem.
   - ❏ Vocabulary: I know words for problems related to marriage, family, and health.

6. Social / Christian Responsibility
   - ❏ I can *read* about a need in another part of the world, and answer questions.
   - ❏ I can *understand* advertising (print and video) requesting charitable donations.
   - ❏ I can *do research* about a missions project or charitable organization.
   - ❏ I can *present* a report on the above, and *answer* questions.
   - ❏ I can *interview* a missionary or volunteer about his or her work.
   - ❏ I can *write* a summary of my interview for a newsletter.
   - ❏ Vocabulary: I know words for natural disasters and social problems.

7. Ethical Dilemmas
   - ❏ I can *read* about ethical issues, and *discuss* my opinion.
   - ❏ I can *participate* in a group decision on an ethical problem.
   - ❏ I can *read* about an ethical problem in our society, and *write* a response.
   - ❏ I can *write and share* a personal point of view on an ethical question.
   - ❏ Vocabulary: I know the words and expressions for controversial issues.

8. Future Plans
   - ❏ I can *understand* a talk about goal-setting.
   - ❏ I can *list* my short and long-term goals.
   - ❏ I can *share* my goals, and *understand* someone else's goals.
   - ❏ I can *speak clearly* about possibilities, probabilities and certainties.
   - ❏ I can *write* a final essay about my goals and dreams, and read it to others.
   - ❏ Vocabulary: I know words and expressions to talk about the future.

9. Christian Content
   - ❏ I can *say* the Ten Commandments.
     Listener: _____
   - ❏ I can *say* Psalm 1.
     Listener: _____
   - ❏ I can *say* Ephesians 6:11-13.
     Listener: _____

Chapter 12

Cross-Cultural Missionary Training and Language Learning: An English Training Program for Korean Christians

Susan Truitt
susan_truitt@hotmail.com

Susan Truitt has been a missionary in Korea with OMS since 1995. She is a professor in the English department at Seoul Theological University, teaching courses in English communication, English education, and second language acquisition. She has a Ph.D. in foreign language education from the University of Texas at Austin.

When missionaries go out to a new area, language learning is usually a priority. What about the increasing number of missionaries from the Two-Thirds World? Not only do they need to learn the heart language of the people on their mission field, but they also often find that their ministry will be more effective in many ways if they can communicate well in English. With English being the lingua franca of today's world, English is an important skill to have for several reasons. One is that language learning materials and courses are geared to English speakers, and missionaries may find themselves learning the target language through English. Before they become fluent in the local language they may also need English to communicate for their daily needs. Finally, English is often the medium of communication between missionaries of various nationalities in a given country. In fact, missionaries who join an international mission agency usually use English to communicate among themselves during training and on the mission field itself.

Missionaries, pastors, and other Christian workers from many nations who are preparing for cross-cultural service are looking for training in English that is specific to their particular needs. This is particularly true in Korea, where about 30 percent of the population is Christian and many missionaries are being sent out.

Missionary training programs for non-native speakers of English may therefore include an English component. For example, at the Korea Evangelical Holiness Church (KEHC) Missionary Training Center, missionary candidates go through a four- to seven-month training program, which includes about four hours a week of English instruction and a two-week intensive English program.

In addition, some Christian universities and seminaries in Korea have departments of "Mission English," which are designed to teach students both English and missions. Seoul Theological University (STU) is one institution with such a department, the goals of which are "first, to train cross-cultural missionaries with theological knowledge and excellence in English which has become the world language and, second, to cultivate Christians who can fill various roles in international society" (STU 2000).

One of the challenges of English programs in a nation like Korea is that even though students have studied English for six to ten years or more in school, they complain that they cannot speak English fluently. Korean students often report experiencing anxiety in using English, particularly in speaking and listening, which may lead them to avoid situations where English is actually used in real communication.

Many Korean English students are therefore searching for a more effective method to learn English. One method is to go abroad and study English in an English-speaking country. This method can be very valuable, but it is expensive and difficult for the average person to have this opportunity. A more practical method for many is to participate in an intensive English program in Korea, where for two or more weeks students can focus entirely on learning English in an environment where English is being spoken all day long, with native speaking English teachers.

Several intensive English programs in Korea have been described, such as the POSTECH Live-in English Program (Dechesne, et al. 1999, Goodwin & Baker 1998) and the English Village Course at Korea Advanced Institute of Science and Technology (Park 1999). The developers have found that these kinds of programs can be effective in improving the students' communicative competence in English. A similar program has been designed for future and potential Korean missionaries, the focus of this chapter.

The "Adventures in English" program

Adventures in English (AIE) is a two-week intensive English program. This program is designed specifically for Korean Christians who want to improve their English ability, with a focus on missionary training. Sponsored by OMS International, KEHC, and STU, AIE has been generally held once a year since 1986. This chapter describes the program based on AIE 2009.

AIE offers Korean Christians a way to improve their English for use on the mission field, for sharing the gospel with English-speaking people in Korea and elsewhere, and for receiving additional education in graduate school. All four skills of English are emphasized: listening, speaking, writing, and reading. Worship, Bible study, outreach, and a variety of other activities provide opportunities to practice English and develop vocabulary. Many of the English materials relate to Christian living, evangelism, and missions.

Twenty-one adults and twenty-six high school students participated in AIE 2009. The adult AIE program ran for two weeks and included some college graduates; however, the majority were students at STU and other universities. The high school AIE program met for only one week. The students were almost all evangelical Christians, though at least two were non-Christians. Students came for a variety of reasons, but most came with at least an interest in missions, and with a desire to improve their English in order to serve God more effectively.

The participants had various levels of English proficiency. They were divided into five groups with about ten in each group, according to their English ability as measured in an interview before the course began.

AIE 2009 ran for two weeks at the end of July, with a two-day break from noon on Saturday to noon on Monday in the middle. From 7 a.m. to 8:30 p.m., the students were required to speak only English. For the daily schedule, see the appendix.

AIE Staffing

One characteristic of AIE and many other intensive English programs is that native-English speaking teachers and/or group leaders are brought in to interact with the participants. This provides opportunities for participants to communicate in English with native speakers without having to leave Korea. In the AIE 2009 program, there were eleven "guides" from the United States. Four of them were full-time English teachers at STU; the others came as short-term missionaries.

The fact that AIE is sponsored by OMS and staffed by volunteers in addition to full-time English professors keeps the tuition cost much lower than other similar English camps in Korea. The program is designed so that the volunteer native-speakers of English can function as guides for the students at AIE, even if they do not have previous experience or training in teaching English, under the supervision and guidance of experienced teachers. These volunteer short-term missionaries arrive in Korea at least one week before AIE begins for a week of orientation to learn some tips on teaching English, prepare for the details of the program, and learn a bit about Korea through sightseeing, church visitation, and a one-night home stay experience.

A ratio of about two guides per group of students enables each guide to have at least one break time during the day when he or she is not responsible for teaching anything; sometimes two guides at a time can be with a group if one lacks confidence or experience in teaching.

AIE Course Content

During AIE, students engage, learn and use English in a variety of settings. Unless otherwise noted, students meet in small groups for these activities. For the schedule, see the Appendix.

Chapel. Chapel was held each morning with all the participants together. Each day a different group of students was in charge of leading the chapel. Each student in the group had to take a part, such as leading the singing, reading the scripture, praying, or giving a sermon.

Culture and Missions. This class was held every morning for an hour and ten minutes. In the class, students read short articles about issues related to Christian missions and culture, and discussed them in English with the teacher.

Bible Study. This class was also held every morning for an hour and ten minutes. In the class, students first read an introductory story that introduced the theme of the Bible study. Then they discussed vocabulary, and read the Bible passage for the day's study. Afterward, they discussed questions about the Bible verses and related the topic to their own lives.

Special Interests. The special interests class was held for one hour each day. Before AIE began, students could choose their preference from four groups: singing, cooking, sports, or pronunciation. Each group used English in its own way to accomplish certain tasks. The singing group, for example, prepared performances for all the participants, while the cooking group made special snacks for all to share.

Chapel/Outreach. This class met for fifty minutes each day. During this time each group prepared to lead the chapel on their assigned day. Secondly, they prepared for the outreach activity on Thursday of the second week.

Conversation. This class met for one hour each day. It focused on helping the students to improve their oral communication skills by discussing everyday topics such as family, jobs, hobbies, etc.

Evening programs. The evening programs were held in the main auditorium with all the participants together. Each evening program began with thirty minutes of singing songs in English. This time was followed by an hour-long special program, either a lecture or activity, followed by discussion in small groups.

Korean prayer meeting. Each evening at 8:30, the students met for a Korean prayer meeting. It was a relief for many to finally be able to use Korean at this time.

Free time. From 9:30 to 10:30 p.m., the students had free time, with the option of going to specified rooms to study or play games.

Outreach Activity. On Thursday afternoon of the second week, each group went out for English outreach. One group went to the Incheon Harbor for personal evangelism with international seamen through Korea Harbor Evangelism. Another group went to Friends of All Nations, a ministry to migrant workers in Korea. A third group went to visit Green Pastures, a Christian community for orphans.

English-Only Rule

The AIE program has an English-only rule, requiring the students to speak only English throughout the program, between 7 a.m. to 8:30 p.m. The purpose of this rule is to give students an "immersion" experience, so that they have a real need to use English for all of their communication needs, as they speak with each other and with the native English speaking teachers/group leaders. Although this is both a benefit and a draw of the program, enforcing this rule effectively has been a problem not only for AIE, but for other programs of its kind in Korea. Students who have never been immersed in an English-speaking setting before feel a great deal of stress when faced with suddenly having to speak only in English all day (Cho 1998, Park 1999). In addition, it feels artificial for Koreans to speak English with each other, when they all speak Korean as a native language.

Various methods of enforcing the English-only rule have been attempted in the past, from monetary fines to singing a song in front of the group to wearing a funny costume for a certain amount of time. One year, the punishment for breaking the rule involved a chart with each participant's name. If someone heard another participant speaking Korean, he or she could put a sticker beside that person's name. At the end of the two weeks, the people with few or no stickers won a prize, while those with the most stickers were asked to help with final clean-up. In AIE 2009, those who spoke Korean had their faces stamped with a funny red picture. Enforcing the rule in a humorous way seems to decrease the stress. However, especially during the second week of the program, as students are becoming more weary, it becomes increasingly difficult to keep them speaking English constantly.

In addition, it should be noted that sometimes use of the students' first language in class is a benefit (Auerbach 1993). Therefore, AIE students are allowed to speak in Korean in limited situations, if the teacher gives permission. For example, Korean may be used in order to more fully explain a concept, to ensure that everyone understands an important announcement, or to prepare for a particular activity. More research needs to be done on the effectiveness of the "English-only" rule in this kind of program, and how to use it appropriately and enforce it effectively.

Results of the Program

In written evaluations given on the last day of the AIE program, many students indicated that their confidence in speaking and listening had increased, and that they were less afraid of speaking with foreigners. Even though their actual English ability may not have improved much in only two weeks, these positive feelings are very important. This will help students continue to improve their English ability after AIE. As one student stated, "This AIE program helped me to improve my English and gave me confidence and courage." Ninety-four percent of the students said that they would recommend AIE to other people.

Beyond the improvement in English, many students stated that they were renewed or challenged in their faith through this program. They reported that they appreciated studying English in a Christian atmosphere, and being able to study the Bible, worship, and do outreach in English. In addition, many students were challenged to think about missions in new and deeper ways and to consider becoming missionaries.

One student stated, "When I entered the AIE program at first, I didn't expect so many things. I just wanted to experience speaking English with foreigners. But as the days went by, I was so impressed with all the schedule, such as missions, Bible study, Korean prayer time, and so on. It was more than to study English only. Maybe the special experience in AIE might be a turning point in my life."

Finally, although AIE is designed not as an evangelistic program but as a training program for Christians, occasionally non-Christians want to attend. In this case, we are careful to explain to them that it is a program designed for Christians, with Christian content focused on missions, worship, and the Bible. If they understand this and still want to attend, we make a decision to allow them to come according to the situation. In 2009 two non-Christians attended AIE in this way, one of them a visitor from China. Both of them seem to have been influenced in a positive way toward Christianity, and the one from Korea has started to attend church.

Conclusion

As more and more Two-Thirds World countries are sending out Christian missionaries around the world, the need for missionary training that is appropriate for their background has increased. In particular, English language training is beneficial for many non-English speaking Christians and missionaries seeking to be effective in cross-cultural communication. Immersion programs, such as the two-week AIE, are one way of providing them with the needed language training along with motivating Christian content.

Appendix
A typical day in AIE

7:00–7:30 a.m.	Chapel
7:30–8:00	Quiet Time
8:00–9:00	Breakfast
9:00–10:10	Culture and Missions Class
10:10–10:30	Break
10:40–11:50	Bible Study
12:00–1:00 p.m.	Lunch
1:00–2:00	Nap/Free Time
2:00–3:00	Special Interest Class
3:00–3:20	Break/Snacks
3:30–4:10	Chapel/Outreach Preparation
4:20–5:20	Recreation or Conversation
5:30–6:20	Dinner
6:30–7:00	Singing
7:00–8:00	Evening Program
8:00–8:30	Food and Fellowship
8:30–9:30	Korean Prayer Meeting
9:30–10:30	Games and Fellowship

ESL Texts Used in this Program

Auerbach, E.R. (1993). Reexamining English only in the ESL classroom. *TESOL Quarterly, 27*(1), 9-32.

Cho, D. (1998). A case study of an immersion English program: POSTECH Live-in English Program. *English Teaching: The Journal of the Korea Association of Teachers of English, 53*(2), 157-178.

Dechesne, M.A., Goodwin, G., Baker, L., & Cho, D. (1999). Operation: Language. *The English Connection: The Newsletter of Korea TESOL, 3*(2), 1, 6-8.

Goodwin, G., & Baker, L. (1998). The POSTECH Live-in English Program: A Language Environment. Proceedings of the 1997 Korea TESOL Conference.

Park, Y. (1999). A study of the implementation of an intensive language course, English Village Course. *English Teaching: The Journal of the Korea Association of Teachers of English, 54*(1), 197-219.

Seoul Theological University. (2000). Seoul Theological University Information Bulletin.

Part B: Materials

Chapter 13

Theme-based ESL Course Design: Theological and Missiological English

Jeannie Chan Yee

A magna cum laude graduate of Yale University, Jeannie Chan Yee received her Masters in Cross-Cultural Studies from Fuller Theological Seminary and her Certificate in TESOL from UCLA. After teaching ESL in various contexts, Jeannie joined the ESL faculty at Fuller from 1998 to 2004 where she developed curriculum, taught, and directed the ESL Program and Writing Center. She also conducted training at TESOL and missionary conferences.

Content-based language learning has proved to be an effective framework for curricular and materials development since it was first described in the 1980s (e.g., Brinton, Snow & Wesche 1989). The noncredit course Theological and Missiological English (TME) is an example of such an approach for high-intermediate level international students in the ESL program at Fuller Theological Seminary in Pasadena, California.[1] In this course, theology is the context in which students develop reading, writing, listening, and speaking skills; English is the tool with which they increase their understanding of theology. Among the many models of content-

---

1   Course prototypes began in the 1990s with teachers Jonathan Washburn, Beth Batchelder and Terri McMahan. The course credits McMahan for her selection of relevant seminary texts. The chapter in this book describes the course as created by the author. Although the course is no longer offered at Fuller Seminary, the editor felt it presented a good model for others, so the chapter is included in this collection.

based language learning, TME is best described as "theme-based ESL."
This chapter describes how five principles for developing a content-based
language course (Diaz-Rico & Weed 1995, p. 118) were applied to create a
course to equip students with the English proficiency, theological competence, and academic skills they need for future theological education.

Principle 1: Plan Curriculum Around Themes

Theology is cognitively and linguistically demanding; however, presenting
themes in a logical progression makes theology accessible to ESL learners.
TME applies this theme-based approach by clustering content along
two broad themes—Who God Is and What He Does. "Who God Is" in
turn breaks down into thematic chunks about God's revelation through
Bibliology (Word), Theology Proper (Trinity), Christology (Christ), and
Pneumatology (the Holy Spirit). Likewise, "What He Does" is unpacked
in units about God's role in Soteriology (salvation), Ecclesiology (the
church), Eschatology (end times), and Missiology (missions).

By learning ESL through theological themes, students more easily
remember clusters of related ideas that build their theological knowledge
base. In addition, themes can be recycled throughout the course. The unit
on Christology, for instance, overlaps with the later study on Soteriology.
Views of the millennium resurface in a discussion on the motivation for
missions. Recycling theme-related vocabulary and concepts throughout
the course allows students to become increasingly competent to
communicate their ideas and to perform language tasks characteristic of
seminary education.

Principle 2: Set Both Language and Content Goals

Goals are set to meet both the specific language demands and theological
knowledge students need to know to function in seminary. Research done
by the course developer—reviewing seminary assignments, downloading
official policies on academic expectations, interviewing professors on
common academic problems, discussing coursework with graduates, even
taking a seminary class—provided a list of the ways language is used to
learn and the kinds of language tasks seminarians perform. For example,
study at Fuller Seminary requires language tasks such as writing papers
with proper citation, participating in small group discussions, reading
1,500 pages per class, and outlining theological arguments. In TME, these
academic language demands are put in the form of language-related goals
such as creating a bibliography, practicing the skill of interrupting, skimming a text, and subordinating ideas from general to specific.

As students practice these language tasks, they concurrently explore theological concepts and thus, can achieve content goals. A content-based course should neither oversimplify concepts nor preclude critical thinking, yet it should be recognized that TME is an introductory level course. It surveys major doctrines so students can understand basic terms, recognize key issues, refute heresy, and apply truths to ministry. Its content goals include concepts in seminary curriculum such as analyzing the nature of God through God's attributes and names, studying church ordinances, and comparing theological views of Christ.

In each unit, doctrines are explored by means of both language and content goals. That is, students work *in* English to strengthen the linguistic skills demanded by theological study (language goals) and work *through* English to comprehend theology (content goals). Figure 1 below illustrates how language goals integrate with content goals to develop academic language skills and access theology.

Doctrine	Language Goal	Content Goal
General Theology	Skim the article "An Evangelical Celebration" to pick out the main ideas of each creedal confession	Based on the article, create one's own definition of what "evangelical" means
Bibliology	Construct arguments and debate the truth of Scripture	Compare and contrast common views of the inspiration of the Bible
Theology Proper	Use listening strategies to take lecture notes on the Trinity	Understand the mystery of the Godhead
Christology	Write a timed essay on the uniqueness of Christ	Explain why Jesus is the only way to God
Ecclesiology	Use context clues to guess the meaning of key theological terms in the text	Identify and understand key concepts of the doctrine of the church
Missiology	Make an outline and construct a bibliography using primary research as well as library and Internet resources on missions	Produce a research report on strategies for missions in one's ministry context

Figure 1: Sample of Integrated Language and Content Goals by Doctrine

Intentional, realistic goals in language use and theological content anchor purpose-driven teaching. Goals focus instruction by concentrating on a particular language skill and theological topic. They help course developers and teachers select materials and learning activities to accomplish these goals. Ultimately, goals measure how well students learned a lesson.

Principle 3: Make Materials User-Friendly

Without ESL support, many international newcomers struggle to decipher theological texts published in English. Like bricks, theological jargon, culture-bound idioms, complex sentence syntax, and various rhetorical styles build a wall of incomprehensibility. However, a three-step ladder of "select, modify, and organize" (Diaz-Rico and Weed 1995, p. 121) overcomes the linguistic barrier to make authentic materials useful.

Select. Locating appropriate materials requires investigating materials students likely encounter in seminary or ministry. Course developers asked professors for course syllabi or bibliographies of introductory courses, browsed the seminary bookstore and library for popular texts, and interviewed international students enrolled in regular classes for their most helpful resources for seminary education. Materials had to meet two criteria: (1) comprehensibility to English language learners, and (2) effectiveness in presenting content goals.

The course's primary text, the *Handbook of Evangelical Theology: A Historical, Biblical, and Contemporary Survey and Review* by Robert Lightner fulfills these criteria. ESL students at a high intermediate to low advanced level generally understand its straightforward prose guided by clear sectional headings. Defining theological vocabulary in context, the book concisely introduces doctrines. Moreover, its balanced treatment of different theological interpretations and discussion questions promote the kind of critical thinking theological study demands.

In addition, the course incorporates an array of authentic materials chosen with language and content goals in mind. Since the course orients students to doctrine, its curriculum includes creedal confessions from various Christian traditions. *Cults and the Occult* by Edmond Gruss offers an intriguing counterpoint to define evangelical faith in relation to heresy. Materials (print, audio, and video) include sermons, articles from scholarly journals and popular Christian magazines, the Bible, primary documents, church ministry tools, mission agency publications, excerpts from seminary texts and curriculum, and Christian authors who write with linguistic and theological clarity. This diversity of materials not only exposes students to a variety of literary genres used in seminary studies but also appeals to different learning styles.

Modify. Making materials user-friendly increases comprehension by presenting content simply but not simplistically. The course adapts selected materials with three critical strategies: dictionary supplements, visual tools, and study guides.

The comprehensive yet succinct *Westminster Dictionary of Theological Terms* by Donald K. McKim broadens students' theological literacy for this course and future seminary classes by providing access to significant theological terms. Sharpening dictionary skills, students scan one-to-three sentence definitions, etymologies, a term's importance, theological meanings, and important Scriptural usage.[2]

Graphic organizers such as diagrams and semantic maps provide further footholds to increase comprehensibility. For example, timelines and event chains visually capture views of the millennium. A graph on justification by grace or works in church history shows trends of soteriology. The sample chart in Figure 2, which walks students through their reading from Lightner pages 14-15, illustrates how text clues and page references can guide students through an authentic passage on theories of biblical inspiration.

Some graphic organizers summarize material; others focus critical thinking or generate ideas on a topic. All enable ESL learners to comprehend content by helping them to visually process authentic materials.

Study guides also accompany authentic materials to improve readability and language skills. The degree of modification stretches student proficiency. At first, extensive study guides for *Handbook* point to paragraph references and ask basic comprehension questions. By the middle of the term, language tasks challenge students to interpret and analyze reading passages. For instance, true or false statements about a chapter require students to articulate reasons and page numbers for their answers. Later, creative and evaluation exercises prompt students to yet higher levels of language processing.

---

2   For more on another good dictionary for ESL students, see this volume, Chapter 22.

Theory *Handbook*, p. 14-15	Characteristics	Evangelical? Yes/No
Natural Inspiration	Bible points to Christ and has many errors; the Word is not objective truth, but becomes true in personal experience	
One Purpose Inspiration	Same as: Writers, acting like typewriters, mechanically wrote down what God dictated to them	
Partial Inspiration	Similar to: Bible is not the Word of God; writers were divinely creative just as Christians today can be	

Figure 2: Chart on Theories of Biblical Inspiration
Directions: Fill in the missing information based on your reading.

Similar study guides are provided when the focus is listening skills. At the beginning of the term, students receive partially completed lecture outlines as they listen to the teacher give a lecture based on the text. As the course concludes, outline props are minimized since students have learned to anticipate main ideas and transition cues.

Organize. If incoherently presented, multiple materials dilute, rather than enhance, content learning. For instance, the Missiology unit draws from over fifteen sources; to help students make sense of them all, materials are organized by major concepts and key questions. The first sequence groups materials by a biblical perspective on missions to discover "Why is mission important?" Similarly, materials are progressively arranged by historical, cultural, and strategic views on missions, each view with its own focus question. Sequencing materials by perspective and asking focus questions allows students to analyze one major concept before learning the next and to form links across perspectives.

The three rungs of selection, adaptation, and organization make authentic materials user-friendly so ESL learners climb forward in their linguistic and theological proficiencies. Even with thoughtful materials preparation, however, the success of language and content acquisition largely hinges on the next principle.

Principle 4: Practice Effective Classroom Instruction

Instruction in TME incorporates communicative teaching principles (see, for example, Richard-Amato 1996), the integration of language skills, and a wide repertoire of techniques (from many sources such as Pollard & Hess 1997 and Brinton & Master 1997).

Each doctrine is explored with in a four-hour weekly unit. In the first two-hour session, learning activities introduce a doctrine along with its core vocabulary. The next two-hour session reviews and expands this knowledge by examining one or two particular doctrinal issues, depending on class interest and language needs.

Session 1. The class begins with a lesson hook to activate student involvement and motivation to study a doctrine. In Class Memory Verses, a student selects and dictates a key verse that identifies the doctrine, for example, 2 Tim. 3:16 for Bibliology. After correcting their written dictation, the class recites it out loud for pronunciation practice. Hymns that sing about theological concepts and Readers' Theatre that uses Bible passages also focus attention. Verbal and written quizzes as well as KWL charts[3] tap prior knowledge (and can be revisited for lesson assessment). Quickspeaks and Quickwrites further connect student experiences with a theological topic. For example, a Quickspeak for Pneumatology asks students to first individually write notes for five minutes on criteria that distinguish if a church is "alive in the Spirit." All students then speak about their respective lists to develop a class consensus. A Quickwrite for Christology prompts pairs to jot answers to "Where would you look in the Bible to show Jesus is God?" Students then form new pairs to discuss responses. From the onset, students practice multiple language skills to prepare for comprehensible input.

The lesson then presents a doctrine's dozen essential words gleaned from the course texts and authentic materials. This specialized vocabulary or "building blocks for Christian theology" (McKim 1996, p. v) empower students to read theological literature and participate in the seminary classroom. Students can access difficult theological vocabulary through a semantic map

---

3   What do we *k*now? *W*ant to know? Have *l*earned? A student volunteer can record class answers as the teacher facilitates input.

that identifies terms and shows their relationships. For example, the parabola in Figure 3 arranges terms chronologically for Soteriology. Students locate terms as they act out the movement of divine descent and ascent (a fun Total Physical Response activity).

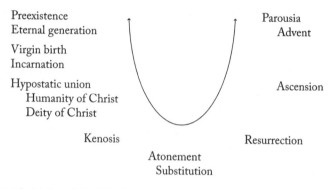

Preexistence
Eternal generation

Virgin birth
Incarnation

Hypostatic union
Humanity of Christ
Deity of Christ

Kenosis

Atonement
Substitution

Parousia
Advent

Ascension

Resurrection

Figure 3: Christology Word Bank

Additional activities recycle these terms to deepen comprehension. Students scan words in a dictionary to paraphrase definitions, find synonyms, and dissect word parts. Alternatively, the class skims a text, underlines theological words, guesses meanings in context, and then creates a semantic map that clusters groups of related ideas. In a pair activity, learners have a post-it sticker of numerous old and new terms on their backs; student A orally describes a term until student B guesses the word. Student A then crosses off the term on a handout, and both circulate to new partners.

The next step before a class overviews a doctrine is for the teacher to prepare students to interact with theological literature. Prediction questions invite them to anticipate a doctrine's themes, controversial issues, or relevance to future seminary classes. A chapter skim highlights headings to orient students to text scope and construction. Noting traits of a theological genre also aids comprehension—a general statement of a doctrine typically uses specialized vocabulary, expository devices, biblical references, and main ideas with details.[4]

---

4   Literature on theological positions includes argumentative devices, assumptions, cause-effect reasoning, and inferences. Materials drawn from ministry-related social science disciplines tend to state a theory backed by examples and testimonies. Church history texts often describe controversies or events that can be understood with *wh-* type questions and attention to chronological developments.

The core of the first class session consists of extended, multiple skill activities with modified, authentic materials. During one week's class, graphic organizers, comprehension questions, and critical thinking tasks help learners access meaning from the text through reading and writing skills. Small group discussions of these reading-writing exercises allow students to test and enrich their understanding from the contributions of others, particularly classmates who are pastors and missionaries. Here, all students practice discussion phrases to give an opinion, pose questions, interrupt, etc. Another week, students first read and write summaries on philosophical and biblical arguments for the existence of God. Then groups roleplay a ministry scenario between an atheist and evangelist, using these proofs of God's reality. In the week on ecclesiology, students play an adaptation of a trivia game. They first read and write notes on materials about the church. The teacher creates comprehension questions from these readings and Bible facts about ecclesiology. As a student reads aloud a question card, the other team answers from their notes and Bible knowledge. Another session uses "the five-minute Professor" (Brinton and Master 1997, p. 283). As the teacher gives a modified lecture based on the text's overview of the doctrine, students write notes. After discussing the content, students reconstruct the lecture and take turns giving portions of it as a mini-lecture or sermon. A final example of an integrated skills activity assigns chapter sections to student groups. Each student makes an outline of his or her section. Members of the same group compare notes to negotiate meaning and create one outline on a transparency or butcher paper to teach the rest of the class. Throughout such cooperative exercises, learning tasks generate reading-writing-listening-speaking connections to work with theological language. Students have repeated opportunities both to process the theological content and strengthen their language skills to communicate in a meaningful context.

Session 2. The second class in a unit advances student knowledge of a doctrine and abilities to perform more complex academic tasks. By examining a particular issue or controversy, students wrestle with difficult questions and use argumentation to express their opinions. For example, in the Bibliology unit, students debate the inerrancy of the Bible or in Ecclesiology, the role of women in church leadership. In other units, students choose a research topic about a doctrine and incorporate analysis and synthesis (over several weeks) to present a report to the class.

Regardless of the assignment, student learning requires explicit instructions and outcomes. To debate the validity of Scripture, teams work on a chart that contrasts evangelical views. A review of argumentative phrases, modeling, guided instruction, and chart cues show students how to develop arguments for or against a position. Clear scaffolds guide students to explain their respective positions, scan materials to find biblical and theological reasons, and draw conclusions from their findings. For the debate, instructions guide students to listen to make rebuttals. Explicit scaffolds for research presentations likewise engage multiple skills. Directions lead students step-by-step to process and express their thoughts, from reading various sources to synthesizing themes across sources. Students also review a public speaking rubric to shape their content and delivery. Later, students are instructed to take notes, evaluate a classmate's speech with the rubric, and prepare a question or share an insight learned. These guidelines, scaffolds, and rubrics help students acquire the language to both comprehend and express themselves around the theological issues. While many teachable moments occur spontaneously, explicit steps lead to increased learning where one extended activity generates multiple skills development and content acquisition.

Principle 5: Evaluate

Frequent comprehension checks throughout a lesson provide feedback on student learning. On-the-spot evaluation identifies language abilities that need more practice or theological concepts that need reteaching. Assessment for each unit as a whole, though, more fully demonstrates how effectively students achieved language and content goals.

The course employs a variety of evaluation tools that measure skills acquired and knowledge learned. They may be traditional, such as the rubric to assess students' oral presentations, or creative, such as a game with team scores. For example, in the Theology Proper unit, a content goal is to understand the Trinity, and a language goal is to increase writing speed under exam-like conditions; thus, the assessment asks students to write one to two paragraphs in twenty minutes explaining how God is One and Three. A survey on Tough Questions Real People Ask especially tests student progress. This tool poses a ministry scenario or problem for each doctrine. At the beginning of the quarter, students mark how well they can answer in their native language. They also mark how effectively they can answer in *English* with a biblical and theological response. After the unit is covered, students revisit that scenario and use lesson concepts to rework their responses in English.

A final assessment, the Statement of Faith paper, requires students to write what they believe and why for each doctrine. This one to two page exercise integrates readings, class discussion, notes, worksheets, Bible knowledge, and individual reflection. For each doctrine, students write a summary paragraph which incorporates a doctrine's key terms to illustrate a general understanding of the doctrine. The next paragraph articulates reasons for a student's view of a controversy. At first, a fill-in-the-blank matrix guides the class. The class also creates a rubric and grades anonymous sample Statements to gain perspective on this challenging task. Later, students write their own statements, peer edit, and revise with teacher feedback. The Statement of Faith paper helps prepare students for language demands of theological study. Students attain academic competence by performing high level language skills, synthesizing unit lessons, and creating meaning from their learning experiences.

Conclusion

TME applies content-based principles to teach Fuller's intermediate ESL students who need stronger academic language skills and a theological foundation for future seminary assignments. Once students' core needs are identified, these principles and related questions can guide curriculum design:

1. Plan Curriculum around Themes
   • What clusters of related ideas make sense of theological content?
2. Set Both Language and Content Goals
   • What specific language tasks and theological knowledge do students need to know to function in seminary?
3. Make Materials User Friendly
   • What modifications progressively move learners toward linguistic independence?
   • What modifications make theological content accessible?
4. Practice Effective Classroom Instruction
   • What explicit scaffolds move students to greater expression?
   • What learning tasks internalize comprehension?
5. Evaluate
   • What activities demonstrate language and content acquisition?

The Appendix illustrates a sample unit that integrates these principles.

Throughout the course, two significant dynamics bring coherence to diverse materials and methodologies: scaffolding and spiraling. Both language tasks and content are scaffolded to accommodate the needs of learners. Students first learn to recognize a topic sentence in a paragraph before summarizing an article. They first learn to make a sentence with a theological term before writing an essay on a doctrine. As students acquire greater proficiency, the language tasks and material become more complex. Similarly with theological input, a word bank forms the foundation to understand a doctrine; an overview of a doctrine in turn serves as a step to examine the doctrine's particular issues.

Furthermore, there are threads which spiral through the curriculum. Within a unit, reading, writing, listening, and speaking activities reinforce comprehension. As students revisit the same theological topic from multiple skills, they retain content. Theological themes across doctrines further connect units; for example, tensions between God's sovereignty and humanity's free will or between conservative and liberal interpretations of Scripture run through numerous doctrinal controversies. Through scaffolding and spiraling, students find the theology more understandable, the English language more useable, and learning more meaningful.

In summary, the synergy of theology and ESL increases the comprehension and expression of theological language. By using English to understand theology, students raise their theological literacy. By using theology to develop English skills, students perform language tasks relevant to theological study. With their improved English and a theological background, students are ready for Fuller's advanced ESL classes. Student comments draw the quarter to an end: "This course was very valuable, as preparation before I will study in the regular program. I got the foundational knowledge of theology and the important terms in English. I knew some different views of each part of theology. I found my position among the different views."

Appendix

Sample Unit on Pneumatology
WEEK 5 DOCTRINE OF THE HOLY SPIRIT
Jeannie Chan Yee, *Theological & Missiological English*, **EL503**
Fuller Theological Seminary, 2000

Topic	Goals	Materials	Activities	Assessment
Theological Words	*Language & Content:* • Identify key theological vocab	• Word Bank	• Word part analysis • Word games	• Make sentences using words in context
Overview of Doctrine	*Language:* • Listen for word bank words • Listen for transition signals • Take notes of live lecture • Interrupt lecturer with verbal phrases *Content:* • Explain what this doctrine means	• Lecture Outline based on chapter 4, *Handbook of Evangelical Theology* (Robert Lightner) • Lecture Comprehension Check Worksheet	• Notetaking • Review & discuss lecture using worksheet	• Evaluate notes using the notetaking rubric • Revise initial answer on Holy Spirit from the course survey
Particular Issue: Spiritual Gifts	*Language:* • Scan for new words • Skim under timed conditions *Content:* • Understand types of spiritual gifts & their applications	• Finding Your Spiritual Gifts Questionnaire (Peter Wagner)	• Inventory of gifts • Discuss how to use one's gifts in ministry • Debate temporary v. permanent gifts using questionnaire, lecture notes, and Bible	• Determine one's gift set

Topic	Goals	Materials	Activities	Assessment
Particular Issue: Student Research	*Language:* • Apply formal speaking skills • Listen for main ideas *Content:* • Research and analyze a topic of interest related to the Holy Spirit • Learn one new insight from each presentation	• Holy Spirit Bibliography for Topical Research Presentations • Samples of previous students' presentation materials	• Speaker: oral presentation for 15-20 minutes • Listener: evaluate speech using public speaking rubric for content and delivery	• Discuss insights learned • Practice error correction for most common linguistic error in presentation
Particular Issue: Holy Spirit in the Church	*Language:* • Read for main ideas, details, inferences, vocabulary in context, and sentence syntax *Content:* • Understand how mainline churches can "quench the Spirit"	• "Father, Son, and . . ." *Christianity Today* (Gordon Fee) • Study guide	• Review questions and compare answers	• Suggest ways churches can be "Spirit-led"
Integration	*Language* *Content:* • Use theological language to write one's view of the nature and work of the Holy Spirit	• Model Statement of Faith on Pneumatology • Samples of previous students' Statements of Faith	• Integrate the unit's reading, notes, discussions, activities, Scripture, and own reflection • Use writing scaffolds	• Write a one-page statement of Faith on Pneumatology

ESL Texts Used in this Program

Brinton, D., & Master, P. (Eds.) (1997). *New ways in content-based instruction.* Alexandria, VA: TESOL.

Diaz-Rico, L. & Weed, K. (1995). *The crosscultural, language, and academic development handbook.* Needham Heights, MA: Allyn & Bacon.

Gruss, E. (2002). *Cults and the occult.* 4th ed. Phillipsburg, NJ: P&R Publishing.

House, H.W. (1992). *Charts of Christian theology & doctrine.* Grand Rapids, MI: Zondervan.

Lightner, R. (1995). *Handbook of evangelical theology: A historical, biblical, and contemporary survey and review.* Grand Rapids, MI: Kregel Publications.

McKim, D. (1996). *Westminster dictionary of theological terms.* Louisville, KY: Westminster John Knox Press.

Pollard, L. & Hess, N. (1997). *Zero prep: ready-to-go activities for the language classroom.* Burlingame, CA: Alta Book Center Publishers.

Richard-Amato, P. (1996). *Making it happen: interaction in the second language classroom.* 2nd ed. White Plains, NY: Longman.

Chapter 14

Content-based ESL Materials: Combining Theology and English

Ethel Azariah
azariah2@msn.com

Ethel Azariah is now retired but taught at Fuller Theological Seminary in Pasadena, CA from 1998 to 2005. Throughout her career in ESL, Ethel also taught at Biola University, at Yonsei University in South Korea, and at a seminary in India. Since retirement, she has taken some short-term jaunts, most recently teaching for six months in North Africa.

Classes for advanced ESL students in seminaries are particularly challenging. Students see ESL requirements as holding them back from seminary studies, yet the reality is that they still need language support and skills development if they are to be successful in their degree programs.

In this context, Fuller Theological Seminary developed a two-level ESL program. It serves master's level School of Theology and School of Intercultural Studies students with internet TOEFL scores ranging between 200 and 237 (533-583 paper-based scores). Students are placed in either the intermediate[1] or advanced level after taking an on-site placement exam. All classes in each level meet two hours a day, two days a week during the ten-week term. This chapter describes the advanced program.[2]

Fuller's advanced ESL course was developed following the adjunct

---

1   See Chapter 13 for a description of the intermediate-level course.

2   This chapter describes the program and materials in place at Fuller in 2003. Thanks to Terri McMahan for developing the first course following this model at Fuller in 1997.

model of content-based language teaching (Brinton, Snow, & Wesche 1989). Students enroll in a four-credit seminary course and a four-credit series of accompanying ESL classes: writing (four credits), reading, listening, and speaking (zero credits each).

The seminary course is one of three different Individualized Distance Learning (IDL) courses. They consist of study guides, four to six required textbooks, a set of audio lectures, and writing assignments. ESL materials have been developed to accompany the IDL courses "Contemporary Culture in Missiological Perspective," "Evangelizing Nominal Christians," and "Biblical Foundations of Mission" so each quarter a different one can be offered. Students find the content motivating, especially since they are getting seminary credit, and the associated ESL classes help them develop the reading, writing, listening, and speaking skills they need as they transition into their regular seminary program. This chapter describes the materials for each of the four skills classes.

Reading

In the reading class, students are expected to increase both their reading speed and their comprehension, in preparation for the heavy reading load they will experience in their seminary courses. Students read the assigned IDL textbooks, covering 150-200 pages per week. In addition, there are two ESL texts.

Scanning. Students are introduced to the skill of rapidly moving their eyes over a page to recognize words and phrases through exercises from a regular ESL textbook, *Intermediate Reading Practices*, by Keith Folse (1993). After they are familiar with the task, however, new materials are used, with words and phrases taken from their IDL reading. Figure 1 shows an example done early in the term with single words. Figure 2, shows a later exercise with phrases. In addition, the teacher may ask students to turn to an actual page from an IDL textbook. She calls out a word and students scan the page to find the word. The first to find the word reads aloud the line in which they found it (a practice which assists students who are still looking). The targeted words are key vocabulary the students should learn.

The first word is the key word. Scan across the row to find the one word that matches it. Circle the matching word and go on to the next key word.

1. segment	figment	segregate	segment	sigmate	cement
2. apostate	apostle	approbate	apostatic	apposite	apostate
3. charisma	character	charred	chasm	charisma	chemise
4. catalyst	cataclysm	catalyst	catechist	castaway	cartilage
5. ethical	ethereal	ethnical	eulogical	ethical	eternal

Figure 1: Word selection drill

Skimming. The skill of reading rapidly to get the main idea of a passage is practiced in the reading class but coordinated with the writing class. The materials consist of reading passages from the IDL texts, about three pages in length, which lend themselves to being summarized. Students are given a time limit for skimming the passage, and writing an outline, which they will later use to write a summary.

Increasing reading speed. Again, students are introduced to this skill with traditional ESL materials. *Timed Readings Plus* (Spargo 1998) includes 400-word readings followed by comprehension questions. Students are encouraged to read these in less and less time. In addition, they try increasing speed with authentic readings (following a suggestion by Anderson 1999). Students are directed to turn to their assigned IDL reading, and read as far as they can in sixty seconds. Then they read again from the beginning, but trying to cover more material the second time. They repeat this three and four times, each time reading more. Their eyes move faster because they are reviewing familiar material before getting into unknown content, and students are encouraged that they can improve their reading rate with real seminary texts.

Improving comprehension. Students are also given materials to develop their skills in finding the main idea, drawing inferences, determining the meaning of words from context, following sequence from transition words, and discerning fact from opinion. Again, the students start with regular ESL materials, in this case, *Timed Readings Plus*. Since there are ten levels in this series, students work at their own level.

Phrase drill. Read the key phrases. Then scan the entire page and circle only the ten key phrases as you find them on the page. The line numbers are for reference only.

Key phrases:

human modesty	historical parallels
classical skepticism	religious dogmatism
moral philosophy	rhetorical analysis
theoretical ambitions	humanistic phase
rational arguments	philosophical inquiries

1. human experience   natural philosophy   intellectual dogmatism

2. reflective Christians   human modesty   secular humanism

3. destructive critiques   transitional phase   classical literature   political assumptions

4. human intellect   humanistic phase   historical assumptions

5. theoretical ambitions   standard account   rational arguments

6. religious dogma   impressionist theory   specific account   philosophical theory

7. theoretical speculations   religious dogmatism   rhetorical analysis

8. classical philosophers   human presumption   honest reporting

9. human cultures   classical skepticism   specific situations   historical parallels

10. moral philosophy   pragmatic demands   modern philosophers

11. specific moments   philosophical inquiries   intellectual methods

12. practical disciplines   theoretical conceptions   practical philosophy

Figure 2: Phrase drill

In addition, students have three sources of theological reading with materials that also develop comprehension skills: IDL texts, journal and magazine articles, and book reviews. First, the IDL course Study Guide contains comprehension questions. Figure 3 gives an example.

1. How has John Donne characterized the beginning of the modern era in his poem?

2. What is the standard account of modernity found in most history and philosophy texts? What contextual factors are missing from this account?

3. How is the concept of a paradigm shift a significant challenge to modernity?

Figure 3: Sample questions from the Study Guide for "Contemporary Culture in Missiological Perspective" (Anderson, G. 2002).

Students are expected to read their text, come to class prepared to discuss the questions in small groups, and refrain from checking the IDL answer key until afterwards. Secondly, the reading class includes a few articles from theological journals or popular Christian magazines on topics related to the IDL course students are taking. During class time, students read the two- to four-page article and answer the questions seen in Figure 4.

1. Who is the intended audience?
2. Whose point of view am I reading?
3. What is the function of this article? (e.g., to inform, to persuade)
4. Are these facts or opinions?
5. What are the presuppositions?
6. What are the inferences?

Figure 4: Standard questions for journal articles.

Thirdly, students practice answering these same questions after reading a book review. The ESL teacher focuses on helping students discern the difference between the author's opinion and the reviewer's opinion. These materials were developed in light of typical difficulties ESL students have in reading seminary assignments.

Writing

The seminary students need to be prepared to write book reviews, essay exams, and term papers. A standard ESL writing textbook, along with activities focused on the kind of writing students will do, is used in this class.

ESL Textbook. Students begin their writing class doing activities from the book *Independent Writing* (O'Donnell & Paiva 1993). This text reviews paragraph writing, covers the steps of writing an essay, teaches how to paraphrase and summarize, and offers sections on "structure review" which students who are weak in grammar can do on their own. After finishing the exercises in this book, students move to writing with IDL content.

Summaries. Each IDL course requires a book report which involves summary writing. Students have already examined book reviews in their reading class, but now look at a review from the writer's perspective. Then they write their own review, following the format designated by one of the Fuller professors (see Figure 5).

BIBLIOGRAPHIC INFORMATION: (Include the title, author, date, and publisher.)

AUTHOR: (Give background information that will be helpful for understanding this book.)

THESIS: (In a brief paragraph, explain the main idea of the book.)

SUMMARY: (Show how the chapters develop or support the thesis.)

IMPORTANCE OF BOOK: (Explain in regard to its field, this course, and your interests.)

RESPONSE: (React to the author's thesis and its development—positively, negatively, or both—in relation to your own opinion, experience, and perspective of the subject matter presented.)

Figure 5: Guidelines for writing a book review (Van Engen 1999)

Essay exams. The essay exam section of the course materials is based on McNamara's (1994) *Work in Progress,* and adapted to the realities of seminary exams. The main types of essay questions (restatement, analysis, and application) are explained and the class is given a list of key words used in essay questions (e.g., *differentiate, evaluate, trace, reflect*). Then students are asked to anticipate the questions that might appear on an exam and write some for their classmates. Each question they write must include a key word from the list and be related to the content they have been studying in their IDL course. Best questions are written on the board and the class determines what type of question they are. Students begin the process of writing their answers by creating a thesis statement in response to the question. The following day, in their Writing Lab (a tutorial context) they choose two questions and write full answers. Sample questions are found in Figure 6.

1. According to Ladd, there are several "ages" in the Kingdom of God. Explain each one and its relation to the others.

2. Trace the motif of "chosen people" through the Old and New Testaments.

3. As recorded in Luke 4, define the "mission of Jesus" and support your definition from the Bible.

Figure 6: Sample student-generated exam questions

Term papers. IDL courses typically require a term paper of 3000 words involving research and application. Figure 7 has excerpts from a sample assignment.

Suggested topics:

- how your church is addressing the issue of alienation
- ways to employ technology for evangelistic purposes in a manner that redeems the technology
- analysis of how your local church body or Christian group has been impacted by the modern/postmodern culture and how it is responding

Instructions for developing the paper:

1. set forth the problem being addressed
2. analyze the response, whether theoretical or practical and the rationale that has been developed
3. critique the whole from a biblical/theological viewpoint
4. propose an alternative approach that is missiologically sound
5. make sure there is a section of creative, proactive, and honest missiological application or integration, not just a quick paragraph at the end
6. use scholarly authorities to document and reinforce your analysis and argument

Figure 7: Sample term paper assignment (Anderson 2002)

To prepare students for this task, the Writing class includes a tour of the Fuller library by the reference librarian, with special attention to on-line research tools. Time in class is also spent on documentation. With a collection of books and journals in the classroom, students create source cards, learning how to identify first and last names, find the copyright date, and recognize subtitles and series titles. Another in-class activity is an exercise in taking notes. Students copy a key paragraph onto a card (paraphrasing will come later), writing its main idea in the top left corner, and its source in the top right. Students later work on sequencing their cards into an outline. For their actual research papers, students will collect and store this information on their computers, setting up folders for each section of the paper. However, in class, not all students have computers, so writing on cards is still a practical exercise.

Listening

Students attend the listening class two hours a week, developing comprehension and note-taking skills. The audio materials from the IDL course form the core of these materials.

Comprehension. Following the model of Lebauer's (1988) *Learn to Listen; Listen to Learn*, a series of exercises have been developed using transcripts of the IDL lectures. Students are given a transcript of a lecture excerpt and first asked to circle words that cue an introduction to a topic. Then they underline instances of paraphrase and repetition. They put parentheses around examples or illustrations, and brackets around any tangents. This helps them attend to these key means of following what a lecturer is saying. Another set of exercises involves prediction, an important skill for comprehension. This time the transcript they are given has words blanked out (Figure 8). As they fill in the words using their knowledge of context and grammar, they are reminded that if they do not immediately catch every word in a lecture, they can still guess what it is. Students are also given a transcript with pieces randomly blanked out (see Figure 9) and told to answer the questions that follow. This demonstrates that even without comprehending every word they can still get the main ideas.

Now later on, the Lausanne _____ for world evangelization began to address the _____ of nominality, particularly alerted to the need, _____, in the west, then, increasingly by many churches in what we now call the majority world. And so the Lausanne Congress, rather one of its working groups, meeting in Thailand, _____ a paper called "Christian Witness to Nominal Christians among Protestant Christians." And this is their definition of _____ which you will find in the syllabus. A nominal protestant Christian is one who within the protestant tradition would call himself/herself a _____, or be so regarded by others, but who has no authentic commitment to Christ, based on personal faith. Such _____ involves a transforming personal relationship with Christ, characterized by such _____ as love, joy, peace, the desire to study the Bible, prayer, _____ with other Christians, a determination to witness faithfully, a deep desire for God's will to be done on earth, and a living hope of heaven to come.

Figure 8. Transcript with blanks.

This typology is in terms of church attendance. Firstly, one who attends church _____ worships devoutly, but who has no personal relationship with Jesus Christ. _____ inline churches, especially, this is either a problem or a fertile mission field, _____ I love to preach the gospel where congregations have not actually heard the g_____ through Calvary, and know little about the victory of Christ, or the impart_____ Christian life and ministry. It's a wonderful opportunity. So there are those _____ regularly, worship devoutly, but who have never heard. B. One who a_____ larly but for cultural reasons only. So I'm here in church because of my natio_____

Figure 9. Transcript with random pieces cut out

Another exercise alerts students to individual lecturer style and the ways speakers convey information. Students are given the chart in Figure 10 while a ten-minute excerpt from an IDL tape is played twice. The first time they think about the information and the second time they complete the chart.

Information type	Pauses	Longer vowels	Re-statement	Paraphrase	Volume	Rhetorical question	Speed
Back-ground information							
Topic announce-ment							
Definition							
Distinctions							
Facts							
Theories							
Character-istics							

Figure 10. Emphasis cue chart

Note-taking. During the second half of the quarter, the class moves to note-taking. Materials consisting of outlines of IDL lectures have been developed, starting with more complete outlines and progressing to skeletons where students must fill in more by themselves. While students listen to excerpts of IDL lectures, they complete the outlines. Before the end of the course, students listen to other lecturers besides the one featured in their IDL course so they can get used to various voices, accents, speeds, and styles.

Speaking

The ESL text *Speaking Solutions* by Matthews (1994) is used because of its good critical thinking and discussion questions as well as a useful chapter on giving a presentation. However, the content is adapted to fit the IDL course.

Discussion. Much of the IDL course-related discussion occurs in the Reading class, but students are prepared for it in the Speaking class. Relevant units in *Speaking Solutions* include "Considering Rights and Obligations," "Judging Ethical Behavior," and "Analyzing a Problem." They include a situation for students to consider followed by discussion questions. Students benefit from the sample phrases provided for each type of discussion and end up using them in their discussions in both the Speaking and Reading classes.

One of the topics for discussion in *Speaking Solutions* is plagiarism. The book includes a questionnaire which is a helpful tool to use while explaining what Americans consider to be plagiarism. Combining that with Fuller's policy on integrity provides for an extremely valuable discussion.

Presentations. After studying the *Speaking Solutions* chapter on presentations, students develop their own presentations based on IDL course content. Presentation skills are also developed as students do impromptu three-minute speeches about a variety of topics and lead the class in devotions (ten minutes maximum, based on a Scripture passage) at the start of each class.

Other speaking activities. Throughout the course, pronunciation is attended to. The teacher may take time during a class session to have students open their Bibles and do listen-and-repeat of biblical names and books of the Bible.

The speaking class is a time when some fun activities can lighten the burden the ESL students carry. One such activity is "messenger and scribe." Two paragraphs of equal length and difficulty are taped to opposite ends of the front wall and labeled A & B. The class is divided into pairs, each working on one of the paragraphs, with one partner seated at a distance from the wall. In each pair, the messenger has the job of going up to the wall, reading the paragraph, holding it in memory as much as possible, and relaying it to the scribe, whose job it is to write it down. The first pair to accurately write the paragraph is the winner.

Finally, ESL students are paired with native speakers of English, usually other Fuller students, to practice conversation for an hour each week. This hour is extremely valuable in helping ESL students fit into the mainstream seminary community, hold a sustained conversation, and learn idiomatic English in a natural setting.

Conclusion

These ESL materials, which include reading, writing, listening, and speaking activities built around the regular seminary IDL materials, are beneficial to students in several ways. First, because they are based on or modeled after good published ESL materials, they really help students develop their language skills. Secondly, because they use seminary content, they are motivating to students. Students also appreciate the efficiency of being able to improve their English while they take a regular course.

ESL Texts Used in this Program

Anderson, G. (2002). *Contemporary culture in missiological perspective.* Course Study Guide based on lectures of Wilbert Shenk. Pasadena, CA: Fuller Theological Seminary.

Anderson, N. (1999). *Exploring second language reading: Issues and strategies.* Boston, MA: Heinle & Heinle.

Brinton, D. M., Snow, M. A., & Wesche, M. B. (1989). *Content-based second language instruction.* Boston, MA: Heinle & Heinle.

Folse, K. (1993). *Intermediate reading practices: Building reading & vocabulary skills.* (rev'd. ed.). Ann Arbor: The University of Michigan Press.

Houghton-Kral, A. (1999). *Evangelizing Nominal Christians.* Course Study Guide based on lectures of Eddie Gibbs. Pasadena, CA: Fuller Theological Seminary.

Lebauer, R. (1994). *Learn to listen, listen to learn.* Englewood Cliffs, NJ: Regents/Prentice Hall.

Matthews, C. (1994). *Speaking solutions.* Englewood Cliffs, NJ: Prentice Hall Regents.

McNamara, M. (1994). *Work in progress.* Boston, MA: Heinle & Heinle.

O'Donnell, T. D., & Paiva, J. L. (1993). *Independent writing.* (2nd ed). Boston, MA: Heinle & Heinle.

Spargo, E. (1998). *Timed readings plus.* Lincolnwood, IL: Jamestown Publishers.

Van Engen, C. (1996). *Biblical Foundations of Mission.* Course Study Guide. Pasadena, CA: Fuller Theological Seminary.

Van Engen, C. (1999). Format for Book Reviews. In J. Brodeen and N. Thomas, (Eds.), *Writing SWM Term Papers* (p. 29). Pasadena, CA: Fuller Theological Seminary.

Chapter 15

Integrating Skills in a Communicative EFL Textbook for Christians

Jan E. Dormer
jan.dormer@gmail.com

Jan Edwards Dormer, Ed.D. has worked in English language
development and seminary education in Brazil and Indonesia since
1995. She currently directs a Master of Education program in
Indonesia, and also teaches at Anderson University in Indiana.

One difficulty ESL or EFL teachers have when searching for Christian
materials is that there is little available that is Christian which also functions as an integrated skills core textbook. Christian materials seem to
fall into other categories: Bible studies, evangelistic materials, or textbooks
limited to building a Christian or theological vocabulary. There are certainly situations in which these types of materials are needed. However,
there are other settings in which basic English is the priority, and materials
must support the development of reading, writing, speaking and listening
skills in English. For example, a seminarian may interact with pastors from
other countries in seminars or workshops, and need basic oral communication skills. Or she/he may want to take part in online discussion boards
on ministry-oriented topics.

Live It![1] is a textbook developed to meet this need for more basic
Christian material for seminary students, in a format which integrates the
skills of reading, writing, speaking and listening, along with grammar and

---

1   An electronic copy of *Live It!* is available at no cost by emailing the writer at
jan.dormer@gmail.com.

vocabulary development. It is an EFL textbook which focuses on Christian topics, assuming no previous knowledge of Christian terminology in English. The title speaks of the abundant life that Christians can live through Jesus Christ, but also of the fact that the book teaches English for general communication: English to be *lived* and used.

In developing this material, I had three main goals:

1) To provide communicative EFL materials for intermediate[2]-level students.
2) To utilize common Christian and church themes.
3) To begin at the beginning in teaching Christian content: to teach the church/Christian culture words and phrases not seen in other Christian English teaching materials.

I had also used many textbooks which did not provide enough practice activities, and wanted teachers using my material to have a source for additional student work. I therefore aligned the grammatical content of *Live It!* with *New Interchange 2*[3], so that teachers could use the *New Interchange* workbook as a companion to *Live It!*

Live It! Content and Format

This textbook contains five units, focusing on topics equally applicable to all Christians, whether training for pastoral leadership or simply involved in lay church ministry. (See the Appendix for a summary of the contents.) The unit titles are:

1) Your Testimony
2) Christian Responsibility in Society
3) Change in the Church
4) Feeding our Bodies and Souls
5) A Missionary's Life

Each unit follows a similar format, including two dialogues, grammar instruction, sections on both general and specifically Christian vocabulary, a reading with pre- and post-reading questions, writing

---

2   Intermediate students have already acquired everyday words and formulaic expressions, and are learning to use more complex grammatical structures to express their own ideas.

3   Richards, J., Hull, J. & Proctor, S. (1997). *New interchange workbook 2: English for international communication.* Cambridge: Cambridge University Press.

assignments, and group work. Each of these sections will be discussed below, with excerpts for illustration.

Dialogues

The core content for each unit is introduced in the dialogues, which are presented in the text and narrated by native speakers of North American English on the accompanying CD. The dialogues introduce both topics and grammatical structures. Teachers can use the dialogues in various ways in a classroom context: to introduce the topic, to provide focused listening practice, and for speaking practice when students ultimately role-play the dialogues themselves. Suggestions for using the dialogues are provided in the teacher's notes at the beginning of the book.

The characters in the dialogues include students, Sunday school teachers, professors, pastors, missionaries, and church members. Following is a sample dialogue between two pastors:

Two pastors meet at a coffee shop to talk. Listen, then practice.

Pastor Don:	Hi Steve! Have you ordered our coffee yet?
Pastor Steve:	Not yet. I was waiting for you. Do you just want the regular?
Pastor Don:	Sure. Nothing else in my life is regular right now, so at least maybe I can have regular coffee!
Pastor Steve:	Let's order, then you can tell me what you mean by that *Waitress . . . We'd like two regular coffees please.* Now . . . what in the world is going on?
Pastor Don:	Well, it actually started about a year ago, I guess, when some of the young people started complaining about the hymns and hymnals.
Pastor Steve:	The singing was too old-fashioned, right?
Pastor Don:	Yeah. Then some of their parents got on their side, saying our worship service was out-of-date and not contemporary enough. They said our church wasn't as exciting as most of the others in town. So, we started singing more choruses, and got a worship team.
Pastor Steve:	And what happened then?
Pastor Don:	Then . . . the older people started complaining that the service wasn't serious enough, and that it was too modern. They said it wasn't as reverent as it used to be. They want to have as many hymns as we used to have.
Pastor Steve:	Well, Don, I can certainly see why your life isn't "regular" right now. It isn't just your church—lots of churches are going through those kinds of changes. The problem is . . . change is hard.

Unit 3: A Time for Change: *Dialogue 1*

Grammar

This book does not provide comprehensive grammar instruction. Rather, certain grammar structures that are often troublesome for intermediate students of English have been selected and highlighted in the dialogues. For example, the dialogue above uses "too" and "enough" in expressing evaluations. It also illustrates common structures for making comparisons. Following the dialogue above, the grammar portion below highlights these points:

EVALUATIONS AND COMPARISONS

Evaluations . . . with adjectives

It's *not* contemporary *enough*.
It's *too* modern.

Evaluations . . . with nouns

There are*n't enough* hymns.
There are *too many* hymns.
There is *too much* noise.

NOTE: Use "many" with countable nouns; Use "much" with uncountable nouns.

Comparisons . . . with adjectives

It's *not as* exciting *as* the others.
Our church is *just as* spiritual *as* theirs.

Comparisons . . . with nouns

My church doesn't have *as many*
choruses *as* yours.

Imagine: John is your neighbor. You invited him to church, but he doesn't want to come. These are his opinions of church. Fill in the blanks, then discuss: What would you say to John?

1. There are _____ many hypocrites in the church.

2. There aren't _____ interesting activities at church.

3. I can be just _____ spiritual _____ you, without going to church.

4. Church is _____ old-fashioned.

5. Preachers ask for too _____ money.

6. Church is _____ as important _____ getting together with my family.

7. There's _____ much praying in church.

Unit 3: A Time for Change: *Grammar*

The introductory "Notes to the Teacher" provide some direction for helping students to discover structures by noticing and underlining certain forms in the dialogue, and similar activities. However, it is recommended that the teacher using this material be equipped to teach the structures highlighted. The grammar segments are not designed to provide complete grammatical explanations for students who have not seen the structures previously. Rather, they are reminders for students who have studied these grammar points in school, but who are not yet using them consistently in conversation.

Vocabulary

One of the primary goals of this material is to teach beginning Christian vocabulary. Each unit teaches words and phrases common to North American Christian culture. Vocabulary is taught in this material both through exposure in the dialogues and readings, and also through focused vocabulary activities. Some vocabulary sections simply present new words or phrases for reference, and others provide specific activities. Two examples of vocabulary sections follow:

CHRISTIAN VOCABULARY

to become a Christian

to get saved
to accept Christ/Jesus
to be born again
to give your life/heart to Jesus
to be converted

Unit 1: Your Testimony: *Vocabulary*

What might you want or need in order to go on a missions trip? Match the phrases, and find out!

Acceptance by a	the country you're visiting
A passport from	then to leave there
A visa from	that are useful to the missionaries
Shots and vaccinations	your country
Clothes to wear,	missionary board or church
Books, toys or other things	as advised by your doctor

Unit 5: A Missionary's Life: *Vocabulary*

Reading

Nearly all seminary students need to develop reading skills. Though this material is not aimed primarily at developing the academic reading ability ultimately needed by seminarians, it can pave the way for longer readings and more academic content.

When change involves language, people often have strong and heartfelt opinions. Read about some churches which had to face linguistic diversity in their congregations.

Vocabulary:

inevitable	*spirituality*	*linguistic*
to refuse	*to urge*	*youth*

Pre-Reading Questions:

1. Read the first sentence of the reading below. What does it mean? Do you agree with this statement?
2. Different cultures view change differently. How does your culture view change? Is change positive or negative?

Reading:

It has been said that the only thing that doesn't change is the fact that there is change. If change is inevitable, why is it so hard for us? Why is it especially hard to accept in the church? Maybe change is hard in the church, because we confuse tradition with spirituality.

Today, people move more than ever before. The immigrant population is increasing in many countries, bringing many linguistic changes. These changes sometimes cause division in churches. Consider these cases:

1. Many Brazilian immigrants began coming to an English-speaking church in the U.S. The Brazilian Christians wanted to start a Portuguese worship service, so that they could bring their non-Christian Brazilian neighbors to Christ. But the church leaders refused, fearing that they would lose control of the church.
2. A German church in Canada was located in an English-speaking area. As the original German members grew older, the pastor wanted to switch to English for the main service, to attract people from the community. However, many of the original German congregation disagreed, and this caused division in the church.
3. A pastor urged a Spanish church in Texas to provide an English service for the youth. The youth spoke English better than Spanish, and wanted to worship in English. The congregation, however, was afraid of losing its Spanish identity. Instead, they lost their youth.

These examples show the high price of misguided traditionalism. There is nothing wrong with tradition itself. But when we refuse to make changes in order to meet people where they are, and bring them to Christ, our tradition has become our god. And the Bible says, "Thou shalt have no other gods before me" (Exodus 20:3).

Post-Reading Questions:

1. Do you think that young people want change more than older people? If so, why do you think this is true?

2. In the last paragraph, you see the phrase, "misguided traditionalism." Write a sentence describing this in your own words. Can you think of any examples of "misguided traditionalism" in your own church or culture?

3. The reading gave three examples of churches faced with decisions about language. Choose one of the situations presented. Imagine that you are a member of that church. Tell what YOU think is the right thing to do!

Unit 3: Change in the Church: *Reading*

Writing Assignments

Though not all seminary students will need to write academic papers in English, most will at some point need the writing skills to at least write an email in English, request information, or share their testimony with a far-away financial supporter. The writing activities in this book can help seminarians develop this type of English writing skill.

Write about a social problem and a solution. Include this information, and your own ideas.

Describe the problem; tell what, why, when, who, where, and how.

Explain your solution.

Tell why this issue is important.

Tell if and how the Church should be involved.

Unit 2: Christian Responsibility in Society: *Writing*

Group Work

The group work provided in this textbook normally comes at the end of the unit, and follows up on key issues raised in the previous sections. It is intended to encourage students to use the language they have learned, as well as form and share opinions on the topics discussed. Following is an example that has students use the English they have learned in a skit.

There are many styles of worship because there are many types of people. Make a skit about one of these situations. Use the grammar structures you learned in this unit!

1. An older woman tries several different churches, and finally finds one she likes.

2. Some young people make a worship service much more exciting.

3. A church that is a "social gathering" becomes spiritual.

Unit 3: Change in the Church: *Group Activity*

Christian Application

Some of the units in this book contain activities which lead students to think about the topic in light of scriptural references. An example is the following activity from Unit 2:

Read Matthew 25:32–41. Answer the questions.

1. Who is Jesus talking to? _____

2. Who is the King? _____

3. Describe the "sheep." _____

4. Describe the "goats." _____

5. In this parable, when we serve others, whom are we really serving? _____

6. In this parable, what happens to the "goats?" _____

7. How does this parable relate to social problems? _____

Unit 2: Christian Responsibility in Society: *Christian Application*

To some readers it may seem as though a book such as this one, intended for seminary students, would include more such exercises than it does. The rationale for limiting these types of Bible study activities is to keep to the original purpose of this text: to provide quality English-learning materials which use Christian content. There is not a lack of Bible study material for English learners. Excellent materials are available elsewhere for this purpose. This material, however, prioritizes the development of English skills over in-depth Bible study.

Summary of Content and Format

Examples have been given here of some of the sections and activities in each of the five units of *Live It!*, providing an overall picture of how the material is organized, and how the exercises are structured.

Though originally developed for seminary students in Brazil, this material has been successfully used in seminaries in Indonesia, Korea and the U.S. as well. For most students, this is the first time they have had an opportunity to talk about issues in the church and in ministry through the medium of English. Some have previously used Bible study materials in English, but most have not used materials which would allow them to develop not only the English language skills necessary for dialogue regarding issues and problems in ministry, but also a deeper understanding of the issues themselves.

It has often been stated that "materials are only as effective as the person using them," and nowhere is this more true than in English language teaching. A capable teacher will be able to use this book as a springboard to creative group and pair work, interesting student presentations, and probing class discussions. When used in such fashion, the material presented in *Live It!* should provide fifty to sixty hours of classroom instruction. This makes it suitable for some semester-long classes. In situations where more classroom hours are provided for English instruction, this material might be used in conjunction with another text focusing on grammar or the development of reading skills.

Conclusion

This chapter has described materials that can be used when seminary students need English for daily life and ministry, not just for academic purposes. It is my prayer that many similar texts be written by Christian English teaching professionals in the coming years, from different theological and cultural perspectives. Perhaps the day will come when English teachers in seminaries have dozens of excellent published texts from which to choose. This is a beginning.

Appendix
Live It! Summary of Content

Unit 1: Your Testimony

Functions:	Self-introductions; exchanging personal information; sharing conversion experiences and spiritual journeys
Grammar:	Past tense; *used to* for habitual actions
Oral Skills:	Discussing past habits; listening to and sharing life stories
Reading:	*The Dramatic Conversion of an Olympic Diver*
Writing:	Writing a personal testimony, or life story

Unit 2: Christian Responsibility in Society

Functions:	Talking about social problems; evaluating current solutions to social problems; asking for and giving information
Grammar:	Adverbs of quantity with countable and uncountable nouns: *too many, too much, not enough, more, fewer, less*; forming indirect questions from Wh-questions
Oral Skills:	Sharing opinions in conversation; focused listening for information; asking for and offering assistance
Reading:	*Meeting the Needs of the Poor in Manila*
Writing:	Writing a description of a social problem and a possible solution

Unit 3: A Time for Change

Functions:	Describing positive and negative features; making comparisons; talking about changes in the church; expressing wishes
Grammar:	Evaluations and comparisons with adjectives: *not . . . enough, too, not as . . . as, as . . . as*; evaluations and comparisons with nouns: *not enough . . . , as many . . . as; wish*

Oral Skills:	Listening to descriptions of churches, listening to comparisons, focused listening for details; giving opinions in conversation; asking questions to discover similarities and differences
Reading:	*The Difficulty in Making Changes in Church*
Writing:	Writing about a wish for a change in your church

Unit 4: Feeding Our Bodies and Souls

Functions:	Talking about physical and spiritual nourishment; expressing likes and dislikes; giving instructions
Grammar:	Simple past vs. present perfect; sequence adverbs: *first, then, next, after that, finally*
Oral Skills:	Listening to a description of a good Bible study method; talking about food preferences
Reading:	*The True Value of a Sermon*
Writing:	Writing about a sequence

Unit 5: A Missionary's Life

Functions:	Describing plans for going on a missions trip; giving advice for missionaries; planning a short-term missions trip
Grammar:	Future with *be going to* and *will*; modals for necessity and suggestion: *(don't) have to, must, need to, had better, ought to, should*
Oral Skills:	Listening to descriptions of missions trips; listening to advice for missionaries; asking and answering questions about necessities and requirements
Reading:	*What are the REAL Requirements for Missionary Service?*
Writing:	Writing a letter requesting action; writing a persuasive paragraph

Chapter 16
Developing Reading Materials for Beginners

Geraldine Ryan
gryan@oms.org.nz

Geraldine Ryan has been serving with OMS International in Moscow since 1997, where she heads the English program at Moscow Evangelical Christian Seminary. She has just finished a Ph.D. in Intercultural Education from Biola University. Her dissertation is titled "Specialized Vocabulary Acquisition Through Texts in the Theology Classroom."

The English program at Moscow Evangelical Christian Seminary (MECS), as mentioned in chapter 8, aims to teach theological English, taking students from a high-beginner level to advanced proficiency in reading. The major challenge has been to find and develop appropriate theological materials for lower levels of English proficiency, particularly given the current trend in second language teaching to use authentic materials. Outlined below is the rationale for, and aims of, the materials chosen. At the end of the chapter is a complete bibliography of all materials used and their approximate levels of proficiency.

Material with Christian content is introduced from the beginning of the program. To ensure that the material is appropriate even at lower levels, two primary principles were followed. The first was to use the students' prior knowledge as a building block and the second was to reduce the input of new data to a manageable level for whatever stage the students are at in their language learning.

The students are started off with a small booklet called *The Life of Christ* (Erny, 1970) which contains adapted stories from the Gospels.

Despite the reading level of the material being high beginner, above the students' level, students are able to read it because of their prior knowledge of the stories. The main emphasis while using these texts is on vocabulary acquisition, since they have a high proportion of the most frequently used biblical words, thus enabling the students to begin to acquire a theological vocabulary early on. The texts are also useful for teaching students to use context and their prior biblical knowledge to help them understand unknown vocabulary. In addition, students want to begin reading Christian material as early as possible and therefore are highly motivated to read these texts.

Although these adapted stories are a good starting point, research into the teaching of reading discourages the use of some adapted or simplified material, citing that simplifying the syntax of a text can actually distort it and make it more difficult to read (Alderson 2000, p.73). For this reason, immediately after *The Life of Christ*, unadapted Christian reading material is introduced. However, initially the content is still very familiar, and the texts are brief, which limits the amount of new vocabulary encountered. The texts come from a set of Bible cards (Grolier 1996), which give brief summaries of such things as Bible characters, events and places. Initially students read cards with familiar material such as characters and events, gradually progressing to the less familiar information about Bible places. The emphasis continues to be primarily on vocabulary acquisition but there is increasing testing of comprehension of both literal and inferred meaning, as well as work on reading skills such as recognizing main ideas and using context. One of these assignments is included as an appendix at the end of the chapter.

The next stage involves reading sections of a chapter from the book *Questions of Life* (Gumbel 1995), which was written as a basic introduction to Christianity for the Alpha course. This particular book and chapter were chosen for two main reasons. Again, a familiar topic—guidance— was chosen so that students bring a high level of prior knowledge to the reading process. Secondly, the chapter is written with six subheadings which easily enables it to be broken down into small assignments to keep the vocabulary load manageable. Three of the six sections are used in class. For the first time students move away from Bible stories to biblical teaching. The goals are now a balance of comprehension work, reading skills development, and vocabulary acquisition.

These three goals continue with increasingly more challenging material. After the assignments on guidance, a few assignments based on short biographies of famous Christians are covered. I wrote these from information gleaned from a Navigator devotional series (CloserWalk) and from a book, *Heroes of the Faith* (Fedele 2003). Although they are slightly simplified and therefore not completely authentic material, I wrote them trying to avoid the distortions Alderson (2000) mentions, and as a result students have no difficulty reading them, and they are of high interest to the students.

At this point students are just over one third of the way through the program, and have had ninety hours of reading. The next group of assignments is from a book written for Christian leaders called *Partners in Prayer* (Maxwell 1996). At this stage of their progress, the book is quite difficult for the students, partly because of the amount of unknown vocabulary, but also because of the high cultural content of the material. (The book is written primarily to encourage church leaders to gather prayer partners to support them, and the American church context in which it is written is, at times, quite different from the church experience of the students. In addition the author uses illustrations and idioms from American culture.) However, the book was partly chosen because students are familiar with the topic of prayer, and the usefulness of the content for future ministry was also a factor, as this increases the interest level of the reading material and the motivation to persevere. I chose to use three complete chapters of the book, divided into smaller assignments, because of evidence that such a practice (compared to many assignments from completely different texts) may help facilitate vocabulary acquisition through both reducing the number of new words encountered, and increasing the frequency of repetition of vocabulary (Kyongho & Nation 1989; Wodinsky & Nation 1988).

The next stage involves students using a theological dictionary as well as learning and using some theological terms. Debbie Dodd's (2003) *Dictionary of Theological Terms in Simplified English* and the accompanying workbook by Cheri Pierson provide ready-made assignments at an appropriate level.[1]

By now students are at a high-intermediate level and the material is transitioning from popular Christian literature to more academic texts. *The Framework of our Faith* (Burgess 2005) is a collection of chapters primarily written by students at Asbury Seminary in the U.S. as a lay person's introduction to theology. As such, it introduces theological vocabulary and concepts but is not written in the dense style of many theological texts. Interestingly, the book also contains quite a large

---

1 See chapter 22 for more on these materials.

number of the words that are part of the Academic Word List (Coxhead 2000); thus it is also useful for teaching that vocabulary.

Assignments based on a chapter from a Bible commentary, *Encountering the New Testament* (Elwell & Yarbrough 1998), are next in the program. Again, the text is not too dense for this level because the commentary is more general, rather than providing the detailed examination of particular passages found in commentaries of individual books of the Bible.

The last two texts are not, strictly speaking, lower-level materials, as they are texts that could be, and are, used in seminary classes. They are used to take the students to the required advanced level of reading. My main criteria in choosing these last two texts were that they be theological in nature and yet interesting for the students to read, introducing ideas that would be new to them. The students are already in their third year of their degree by the time they get to this level in their English classes and have already studied a lot of theology in their seminary courses. Therefore systematic theology that they would have studied in Russian would not be of interest to them. *Let's Start with Jesus* (Kinlaw 2005) is theological in nature but also concerned with spiritual development. Students enjoy the applied theology. *Announcing the Kingdom* (Glasser 2003) is concerned with the theology of mission, another new area for them.

In developing this lower-level material I relied on four books in particular for both a theoretical basis and for ideas for actual exercises. *Vocabulary in Language Teaching* (Schmitt 2000), *How to Teach Vocabulary* (Thornbury 2002), and *Learning Vocabulary in Another Language* (Nation 2001) informed the way I developed materials for vocabulary acquisition. For reading, I used *Developing Reading Skills* (Grellet 1981). In addition, a wide range of ESL textbooks teaching reading skills were examined for ideas.

With regard to vocabulary acquisition, two primary principles were followed. The first was to ensure that students have to make plenty of decisions about new vocabulary. Schmitt (2000, p.121) says that the more one manipulates, thinks about and uses a word the more it will be remembered, while Nation (2001, p. 63) outlines three processes which he believes are important to ensure that words are remembered. Those three processes are noticing, retrieving and creative (generative) use of a word. Retrieving means doing tasks where the word has to be retrieved from memory, and creative use means using a word in different ways. Thus, the vocabulary exercises in my assignments require the students to retrieve the right word in a different context and use it in some new way. The second principal was to ensure words are recycled, as repetition is also very important for vocabulary learning. The general pattern is that first the words the students will come across in the text are listed with a Russian translation. Students then complete a series of exercises where they have to use the new words and make choices about them. Some of these are done before the students read the text, which may help them to notice and remember the word when they read it, but most are completed for homework after reading the text in class, thus ensuring the students have already met the words in context. Words are recycled through such exercises as giving definitions of previously introduced words and having students find them in the present text, as well as frequent vocabulary games, quizzes and dictionary exercises.

In deciding which words to focus on, in addition to theological and biblical vocabulary, reference was made to the 2,000 most common words in English, known as the General Service List (West 1953) and to the Academic Word List (Coxhead 2000). A number of scholars in the field of vocabulary acquisition (e.g., Nation 2001; Nagy 1997; Laufer 2005) advocate the explicit teaching of these words in the ESOL classroom. I agree that this is particularly necessary in an EFL context where the students have little opportunity to use English outside of the classroom, and in an academic context where they also have little time to do the extensive reading of English that is needed to acquire vocabulary incidentally. Over the course of my reading program students are explicitly introduced to the majority of the 2,000 most common words in English, approximately two thirds of the 570-word Academic Word List (AWL) and about 300 biblical and theological word families and phrases. However, a number of AWL and theological words are very similar in Russian so do not need explicit instruction in the classroom.

A wide range of reading skills are covered over the course of all the assignments, but particular attention is given to using context, identifying main ideas and recognition of word parts, such as the meaning of prefixes and common basewords. It should be noted though, that standard ESL reading skills material is used throughout the course to supplement the Christian material. These texts, such as the *Reading Power* series (Mikulecky & Jeffries 1997, 1998), and *Beginning Reading Practices* (Folse 1993), are where much of the reading skills instruction occurs.

To conclude, authentic texts were used as much as possible in the development of these lower-level materials. Drawing on prior knowledge and reducing the input of new data helped to ensure those authentic texts could still be read at lower levels.

Appendix
Sample ESL Materials for use with Grolier Bible Cards

Jerusalem[2]

1. Pre-reading discussion
What do you know about Jerusalem, e.g., who made it the capital of Israel?
Which empires destroyed Jerusalem? What events in the gospels took place
there?

2. Vocabulary
(i) [with Russian translations]
dry (adj)
sole (adj)
source (n)
spring (n)
crossing (n)
trade (n)
to exist (v)
walled (adj)
to capture (v)
to increase (v)
to strengthen (v)
defenses (n)
to destroy (v) [to be destroyed – *passive*]
siege (n)
fortress (n)
moat (n)
sumptuous (adj)
to suffer (v)
to bury (v)

(ii) *Complete the sentences with words from the list. Remember to use the*
correct tense form if the word is a verb.
    1.   Atheists don't believe that God _____.
    2.   The police _____ the terrorists and sent them to
        prison.

---

2   The actual text from the Grolier card has not been included because of copyright reasons.

3. When countries buy and sell products with other countries they _____ with each other.
4. Prices of food have _____ a lot in the last five years.
5. We are having very _____ weather at the moment. It hasn't rained for weeks.
6. Jesus _____ and died on the Cross.
7. In World War Two, the _____ of Leningrad lasted for three years.
8. The city's _____ were not strong so they were easily defeated.
9. The Babylonians _____ Jerusalem in 587 BC.
10. The dog _____ his bone in the ground.

(iii) *In your vocabulary list is the verb 'to strengthen'. In the table below are other 'measurement' verbs. Look at the sentences that follow and use them to fill in the noun and adjective forms of these verbs.*

Verb	Noun	Adjective
to strengthen		
to lengthen		
to widen		
to deepen		

- George is very strong. He has a lot of strength in his arms.
- An Olympic stadium is very long. In the first Olympics, people ran a race the length of the stadium.
- My street is twenty meters wide. Its width is twenty meters.
- That river is fifteen meters deep. Its depth is fifteen meters.

1. What is the suffix on all the verbs?
2. What is the ending on all the nouns?
3. The verbs 'to strengthen' and 'to lengthen' are formed from the _____. (*What part of speech?*)
4. The verbs 'to widen' and 'to deepen' are formed from the _____.

(iv) *Vocabulary Review: Find words in the text that mean the following:*
1. to go completely around something (paragraph 1)
2. to make something by putting pieces together (paragraph 2)
3. to continue in the same condition (paragraph 4)

3. Comprehension
Read the text again.

a. *Use information from the text to complete the following timeline. Write a sentence beside each date about Jerusalem at that time. (The first date has been done for you.)*

2000 BC   -   Jerusalem was a small walled city

1000 BC   -

10ᵗʰ C BC   -

8ᵗʰ C BC   -

587 BC   -

37 BC   -

70 AD   -

b. *Use the text to decide if these sentences are true or false. (Write T or F beside them.) For the sentences that are false, write true sentences below.*

1. Jerusalem is on flat land.
2. There is not much rain in the region around Jerusalem.
3. Jerusalem is in a good location for trade.
4. Jerusalem was originally a Canaanite city.
5. King David built a bigger city after he captured it.
6. King Hezekiah built a new spring.
7. The Greeks ruled Jerusalem for a time.
8. King Herod the Great increased the size of the city.
9. Roman soldiers lived in a camp in Jerusalem after the city was destroyed in AD 70.

Materials Used in the ESL Program

Bible cards. (1996). Danbury, CT: Grolier Inc. (high-beginner/low-intermediate level)

Biographies adapted from *Closer walk.* Colorado Springs: The Navigators, and Fedele, G. (2003). *Heroes of the faith.* Gainsville, FL: Bridge-Logos. (intermediate level)

Burgess, H.W. (2005). *The framework of our faith: The basics of knowing Christ.* Anderson, IN: Bristol House. (high-intermediate level)

Dodd, D. and C. Pierson. (2003). *Dictionary of theological terms in simplified English & student workbook.* Wheaton, IL: Evangelism and Missions Information Service (EMIS). (intermediate level)

Elwell, W. and R. Yarbrough. (1998). *Encountering the New Testament.* Grand Rapids, MI: Baker Book House. (high-intermediate level)

Erny, E. (1970) *The life of Christ.* Republic of China: Chung Tai English Ministries. (high-beginner level)

Glasser, A.F. (2003). *Announcing the kingdom.* Grand Rapids, MI: Baker. (advanced level)

Gumbel, Nicky. (1995). *Questions of life.* 2nd ed. Sussex, England: Kingsway Publications. (intermediate level)

Kinlaw, D.F. (2005). *Let's start with Jesus.* Grand Rapids, MI: Zondervan. (high-intermediate/advanced level)

Maxwell, J. (1996). *Partners in prayer.* Nashville, TN: Thomas Nelson. (intermediate level)

ESL Texts Used in this Program

Alderson, J. C. (2000). *Assessing reading.* Cambridge: Cambridge University Press.

Coxhead, A. (2000). A new academic word list. *TESOL Quarterly, 34*(2), 213-238.

Folse, K. (1993). *Beginning reading practices* (rev'd ed.). Ann Arbor, MI: The University of Michigan Press.

Grellet, F. (1981). *Developing reading skills.* Cambridge: Cambridge University Press.

Kyongho, H. & Nation, P. (1989). Reducing the vocabulary load and encouraging vocabulary learning through reading newspapers. *Reading in a Foreign Language, 6*(1), 323-335.

Laufer, B. (2005). Focus on form in second language vocabulary learning. *EUROSLA Yearbook, 5,* 223-250.

Mikulecky, B. & L. Jeffries. (1997). *Basic reading power*. New York: Addison Wesley Longman.

Mikulecky, B. & L. Jeffries. (1998). *Reading power*. New York: Addison Wesley Longman.

Nagy, W. (1997). On the role of context in first- and second-language vocabulary learning. In N. Schmitt, & M. McCarthy (Eds.), *Vocabulary: Description, acquisition and pedagogy* (pp. 64-83). Cambridge: Cambridge University Press.

Nation, I. S. P. (2001). *Learning vocabulary in another language*. Cambridge: Cambridge University Press.

Schmitt, N. (2000). *Vocabulary in language teaching*. Cambridge: Cambridge University Press.

Thornbury, S. (2002). *How to teach vocabulary*. Essex: Pearson Longman.

West, M. (1953). *A general service list of English words*. London: Longman.

Wodinsky, M. & Nation, I.S.P. (1988). Learning from graded readers. *Reading in a Foreign Language, 5*(1), 155-161.

Chapter 17
Extensive Reading Materials for Pre-Seminary ESL Students

Nancy Schoenfeld
nance4jc@juno.com

Nancy Schoenfeld is an English language instructor at Kuwait University.
She has an M.A. degree in TESOL from Biola University. Her research
interests are teaching second language reading and vocabulary and she
has done teacher training both in the U.S. and in Indonesia.

Seminary students typically have very heavy reading loads and one of the
challenges for non-native English students is how to build the vocabulary
and reading skills necessary to handle such a load. An approach that has
been shown to be effective is extensive reading (Day & Bamford 1998).
This involves reading large amounts of text at or below the student's current
reading level. The emphasis is on fluently reading materials that individual
students themselves choose, based on personal interests. Extensive reading can improve students' reading speeds and comprehension, provide
input for vocabulary learning, and build confidence (see Walker 1997 for a
further description of these and other benefits).

This approach, however, requires materials. Most extensive reading
programs use "graded readers," which typically come in up to six levels,
depending on the publisher, using a vocabulary which ranges from 200
to 5,000 words. Many of these readers are versions of literary classics
whose plots have been simplified and lexis and syntax controlled. Others
are written especially for ESL students. Unfortunately, as I found while

teaching in the intensive English program at Biola University,[1] the content of these readers—whether classic or popular fiction—is not always appealing to academically-minded students who are preparing for theological seminary. They may think it a waste of time to read a simplified version of *A Tale of Two Cities* or may see a horror or romance novel as questionable for a Christian. Convinced that with suitable materials seminary-bound students could benefit from extensive reading, I looked for a way to locate and select texts.

As far as content, it was clear that texts used in seminaries or explicitly Christian books would not only be motivating to students but would help build their background knowledge in English to assist future comprehension. But since extensive reading is premised on the fact that students need to read at or below their current comprehension level, I needed a way to assess the difficulty of texts.

Assessing Text Difficulty

Although comprehension is affected by many factors (including content, discourse, and syntax), one major factor that is relatively easy to measure is vocabulary. In other words, if there are a lot of unknown words in a text, it will be harder to read. The research of Paul Nation (2001) offered both a framework for and the means of selecting texts based on lexical difficulty. Nation claims that if the goal is for students to develop fluency in reading, that is, simply increase their speed, they should be reading texts where they know 99-100 percent of the words on the page. A second goal of extensive reading is language growth. Here, students are developing reading skills in general and learning vocabulary along the way. This can occur when students know 95-98 percent of the words on the page. Figure 1 summarizes this.

The bottom line is that for language growth to occur through extensive reading, texts should have at most five unfamiliar words for every hundred words of text, or two lines of text for every unfamiliar word—that's what "95 percent coverage" means.

Computer programs have made it relatively easy to determine cover-age. Nation has a vocabulary Range program available on his website: http://www.victoria.ac.nz/lals/staff/paul-nation/nation.aspx.[2] What follows is a description of how I used this program to assess texts for their difficulty as a precursor to developing an extensive reading

---

1   This program is described in Chapter 1.

2   Be sure to follow his instructions carefully!

program for seminary-bound students. My hope is that this will not only give readers specific information about the difficulty of certain texts, but will encourage them to use Nation's or a similar program to evaluate books of interest and value to their students.

Extensive reading goal	Number of unfamiliar words per one hundred words in the text	Number of text lines per one unfamiliar word	Percent of text coverage
Fluency development	1	10	99 percent
Language growth: best	2	5	98 percent
Language growth: possible	5	2	95 percent
Not suitable for extensive reading	10	1	90 percent

Figure 1: Lexical Unfamiliarity for Extensive Reading Goals (Adapted from Nation 2001, p. 150)

At first I wanted to see how difficult actual seminary texts were. I found six classes required by all students in Talbot Theological Seminary, regardless of program or major, and located the eleven texts required for these classes. The classes included Hermeneutics/ Bible Study Methods, Personal Foundations of Ministry, Survey of Matthew-Revelation, and Reformation/Modern Theology. I scanned at least one chapter and sometimes up to four consecutive chapters from each text,[3] that is between 200,000 and 250,000 words,[4] and ran Nation's Range program. A sample of what the program reveals and the coverage of the text from Gundry's *A Survey of the New Testament* is found in Figure 2.

List One consists of the thousand most frequent words in English. List Two is the second thousand most frequent words.[5] List Three consists of the 570 most common academic words as compiled by Coxhead

---

3   For a complete list of texts and results, see Appendix A.

4   The length of the chapters varied greatly between texts.

5   These frequencies are from West's General Service List of words. Details are found in Nation (2001).

(2000) in her Academic Word List (AWL).[6] Proper nouns, of course, are counted separately. The last category, "not on any lists," means that the words did not come from any of the previous lists. These would include specialized and technical vocabulary particular to the text's subject area. Assuming that an intermediate/advanced ESL learner knows the words in Lists One through Three, and is not troubled by proper nouns, it is the last category which is "unknown." Thus, Gundry has 12.2 percent unknown words, or 87.8 percent coverage. This means that this text is too difficult to be considered for extensive reading purposes.

List	Number/percentage of unique words	Coverage
Words from List One — 1st 1000	8819 / 70.0 percent	
Words from List Two —2nd 1000	744 / 5.9 percent	
Words from List Three — AWL	554 / 4.4 percent	Coverage = 87.8 percent
Proper nouns	930 / 7.4 percent	
Words not on any lists	1547 / 12.2 percent	

Figure 2: Lexical analysis of Gundry's *A Survey of the New Testament.*

Of the eleven texts I scanned, only two were close to qualifying for extensive reading. *Changes that Heal* by Cloud had 94.6 percent coverage. 89.7 percent of its words were from Lists One and Two, 2.6 percent were from List Three (the AWL), 2.3 percent were proper nouns, and 5.3 percent were not on any lists. Grudem's *Systematic Theology* also had 94.6 percent coverage. 84.3 percent of its words were on Lists One and Two, 4.6 percent were academic vocabulary from List Three, 5.8 percent were proper nouns, and 5.3 percent were not on any lists. Note that although Grudem and Cloud have a similar percentage of words not on any list, Grudem has more academic vocabulary and proper nouns, so it may be more difficult to read.

6   Go to http://www.victoria.ac.nz/lals/staff/Averil-Coxhead/awl/headwords. html for an explanation of how the Academic Word List (AWL) was compiled and for an explanation of its construction and use.

Suitable Texts

My next step was to look for books that might more realistically be suitable for extensive reading for seminary-bound students. Since lexical analysis is time-consuming, it is sensible to undertake it only with the expectation that one will get good results. The next genre I considered was Christian middle and high school Bible curriculum texts. I assessed a textbook from Bob Jones' University Press Bible Modular Series, *That I May Know Him* (Garland, 2002). Coverage was 94.4 percent, close to the goal of 95 percent. (Details can be found in Appendix A.) Readability in these books and others written for American teens is also enhanced by pictures and graphics, though visuals may make adults feel patronized.

It should be noted that besides the benefits of Christian content, which motivates seminary-bound students to engage in the extensive reading program, the theological books contain more academic vocabulary (List Three) than traditional graded readers. Developing increased familiarity with academic vocabulary is an important step for all academic ESL students, regardless of their specific discipline. In fact, some studies have shown that general academic vocabulary is more troublesome than discipline-specific vocabulary.[7]

At the same time, fiction can be engaging to students. Since the benefits of extensive reading accrue simply when students read a lot, whatever holds a student's interest will be a good addition to the extensive reading library. For that reason I examined the first book in the popular *Left Behind: The Kids* series. Total coverage was 95.5 percent, making it lexically accessible. (As expected, only 0.9 percent of the words were academic, from List Three.)

These positive results for a teen series led me to investigate other Christian books for teens. I examined both the original and the student versions of Strobel's *The Case for Christ*. Although the teen version (93.7 percent coverage) would be less lexically challenging than the original (92.3 percent coverage), it still didn't hit the target number for extensive reading. This is a good reminder of the value of the running the program to check intuition.

So far, the discussion has focused on using authentic texts, that is, texts written for native speakers. However, I'd also like to point out some theological materials written in English, especially for non-native speakers. Wycliffe Bible Translators, to serve the growing number of

---

7   Cohen, Glasman, Rosenbaum-Cohen & Fine (1988) and Anderson (1980) cited in Nation (2001) pg. 190.

their translators who do not speak English as their native language, has published Bible commentaries and other resources in what they call "easy English." These are available at www.easyenglish.info. I examined seven commentaries and they ranged in coverage from 95.7 percent (Luke) to 97.9 percent (James).[8] For interested students, these are good candidates for extensive reading, especially for purposes of building fluency.

It has proved difficult to find Christian texts appealing to seminary-bound students which have 98 percent or higher coverage. Thus, students who need to build reading fluency, particularly those at intermediate and lower levels, may need to make do with the regular graded readers for ESL learners. However, we can be encouraged that there are lexically accessible texts for intermediate and advanced students who can use materials with 95 percent coverage for language growth. These may include materials published for both adults and teens, so long as they have face validity for graduate-level students eager to prepare for seminary studies.

Teachers who want their students to reap the benefits of extensive reading can look for a variety of Christian fiction and non-fiction. Using Nation's Range program we can determine whether these books qualify for reading fluency or language growth, or whether they are best used for intensive classroom work rather than extensive reading.

---

8   See Appendix B for more results.

Appendix A
Text Analysis Results of Selected Texts

List	Number/percentage of unique words	Coverage
One	8819 / 70.0 percent	
Two	744 / 5.9 percent	
Three	554 / 4.4 percent	87.8 percent
Proper nouns	930 / 7.4 percent	
Not on any lists	1547 / 12.2 percent	

Gundry, R.H. 1994. *A Survey of the New Testament* (3rd ed.).

List	Number/percentage of unique words	Coverage
One	10914 / 84.0 percent	
Two	743 / 5.7 percent	
Three	340 / 2.6 percent	
Proper nouns	298 / 2.3 percent	94.6 percent
Not on any lists	693 / 5.3 percent	

Cloud, H. 1992. *Changes that Heal.*

List	Number/percentage of unique words	Coverage
One	10578 / 81.5 percent	
Two	364 / 2.8 percent	
Three	599 / 4.6 percent	
Proper nouns	761 / 5.8 percent	94.6 percent
Not on any lists	673 / 5.3 percent	

Grudem, W. 1994. *Systematic Theology: An Introduction to Biblical Doctrine.*

List	Number/percentage of unique words	Coverage
One	5310 / 81.2 percent	
Two	266 / 4.1 percent	
Three	204 / 3.1 percent	
Proper nouns	395 / 6 percent	94.4 percent
Not on any lists	365 / 5.6 percent	

Garland, H.D. 2002. *That I May Know Him.*

List	Number/percentage of unique words	Coverage
One	4933 / 85.5 percent	
Two	319 / 5.5 percent	
Three	52 / .9 percent	
Proper nouns	202 / 3.5 percent	95.5 percent
Not on any lists	261 / 4.5 percent	

Jenkins, J.B., & LaHaye, T. 1998. *Left Behind the Kids: The Vanishing.*

List	Number/percentage of unique words	Coverage
One	5217 / 77.8 percent	
Two	251 / 3.7 percent	
Three	310 / 4.6 percent	
Proper nouns	415 / 6.2 percent	92.3 percent
Not on any lists	514 / 7.7 percent	

Strobel, L. 1998. *The Case for Christ.*

List	Number/percentage of unique words	Coverage
One	4790 / 82.2 percent	
Two	209 / 3.6 percent	
Three	152 / 2.6 percent	93.7 percent
Proper nouns	307 / 5.3 percent	
Not on any lists	371 / 6.3 percent	

Strobel, L., & Vogel, J. 2001. *The Case for Christ: Student Edition.*

Appendix B
Text Analysis of On-line Easy English Commentaries

Book	Total coverage
Hebrews	97.8 percent
Jonah	97.5 percent
James	97.9 percent
1 Peter	97.3 percent
Jude	97.6 percent
Philippines	97.4 percent
Luke	95.7 percent

www.easyenglish.info

ESL Texts Used in this Program

Blomberg, C.L. (1997). *Jesus and the gospels: An introduction and survey.* Nashville, TN: Broadman and Holman Publishers.

Cairns, E.E. (1996). *Christianity through the centuries.* (3rd ed.). Grand Rapids, MI: Zondervan.

Cloud, H. (1992). *Changes that heal.* Grand Rapids, MI: Zondervan.

Coxhead, A. (2000). A new academic word list. *TESOL Quarterly, 34,* 213-238.

Crabb, L. (1998). *Inside out* (2nd ed.). Colorado Springs, CO: Navpress.

Day, R.R., & Bamford, J. (1998). *Extensive reading in the second language classroom.* Cambridge: Cambridge University Press.

Garland, H.D. (2002). *That I may know Him.* Greenville, SC: Bob Jones University Press.

Grudem, W. (1994). *Systematic theology: An introduction to biblical doctrine.* Leicester, England: Intervarsity Press.

Gundry, R.H. (1994). *A survey of the New Testament* (3rd ed.) Grand Rapids, MI: Zondervan.

Jantz, G., & A. McMurray. (1999). *Too close to the flame.* West Monroe, LA: Howard Publishing.

Jenkins, J.B., & LaHaye, T. (1998). *Left behind the kids: The vanishing.* Wheaton, IL: Tyndale House.

Klein, W.W., Blomberg, C.L., & Hubbard, R.L. (1993). *Introduction to biblical interpretation.* Dallas, TX: Word Publishing.

Moreland, J.P., & Reynolds, J.M. (Eds.). (1999). *Three views of creation and evolution.* Grand Rapids, MI: Zondervan.

Nation, I.S.P. (2001). *Learning vocabulary in another language.* Cambridge: Cambridge University Press.

Nation, I.S.P., & Heatley, A. (1996). *VocabProfile, Word, and Range: Programs for processing text.* New Zealand: LALS, Victoria University of Wellington.

Plantinga, C., Jr. (1995). *Not the way it's supposed to be: A breviary of sin.* Grand Rapids, MI: William B. Eerdmans.

Russell, W. (2000). *Playing with fire: How the Bible ignites change in your soul.* Colorado Springs, CO: Navpress.

Strobel, L. (1998). *The case for Christ.* Grand Rapids, MI: Zondervan.

Strobel, L., & Vogel, J. (2001). *The case for Christ: Student edition.* Grand Rapids, MI: Zondervan.

Walker, C. (1997). A self access extensive reading project using graded readers (with particular reference to students of English for academic purposes). *Reading in Foreign Language, 11,* 121-149.

Chapter 18
Content-based Academic Listening: Biola University's Theological English Through Video Series

Peggy Burke
peggy.burke@biola.edu

Peggy Burke, Ph.D., Associate Professor, teaches English as a
Second Language in the English Language Studies Program at Biola
University, La Mirada, California.

Some time back I was teaching a lecture-listening course to students in
Biola University's English Language Studies Program (ELSP).[1] Most
of the students, largely Korean, were preparing to enter Talbot School of
Theology as soon as they had attained an adequate level of English. Sure,
the students were learning the requisite note-taking skills, but the content of the lectures—on topics ranging from the environment to women's
rights—was not engaging to them. It was the lecture on sharks, however,
that was the *coup de grace*. For a group of international pastors who were
spending precious time and money in the U.S. and had cast a wistful eye at
the distant land of Talbot only two hundred yards, but two long semesters,
away—the shark lecture was the last straw. We simply had to give them
something more meaningful as they developed their language skills.

Since the students longed for Talbot studies, why not video some
Talbot professors, and then use the videos in our classes? This chapter
describes the development of the *Theological English through Video Series*.

---

1   See chapter 1 for more on this program.

The purpose is not only to describe these materials, which may be of use to other seminary ESL programs, but also to provide insight into the materials development process, including interdepartmental dynamics, that are essential to making a project of this nature a reality.

Materials Development

One of the factors leading to the success of this project was the good working relationship between ELSP and Talbot Seminary. The Dean of Talbot, together with the entire Talbot faculty, could not possibly have been more supportive. Another key to success was the support of the ELSP administration and staff, including our dean, who approved the budget; our program director; and our administrative assistant, who took care of the detail work (e-mail correspondence, scheduling, honorarium payments to lecturers, arranging classroom setup, etc.). Finally, the project could not have succeeded without the help of the Communications Department at Biola, who provided a project manager with expertise in cinematography and editing.[2]

Initially, we had thought of just asking for permission to come into classes and tape segments of regular courses, but the project manager suggested that short, self-contained mini-lectures would be better. In this way we would have more control over the lighting and quality of the production. In addition, short lectures would be better for ESL learners. Thus, we invited participation in what we called the "Fifteen-Minutes-of-Fame Lectures," in which professors could select a favorite topic or portion of a class and present it as a short, self-contained unit, filmed in front of a live audience. In order to have a variety of disciplines represented, e.g., Old and New Testament, Historical Theology, Biblical Theology, Christian Education, and even Philosophy and Apologetics, we e-mailed selected professors inviting them to participate.

The Talbot professors who accepted the invitation were provided with guidelines, which included suggestions for speaking to an ESL audience. For instance, they should speak at natural speed without glossing the language, but be sure to define new terms. They should outline their material and provide visual support. Fifteen minutes was merely a general

---

2   Thanks to the following who were in these positions at the time of the materials development: Ed Norman, Dean of the School of Professional Studies; Sung Lee, ELSP Program Director; Dennis Dirks, Administrative Dean of Talbot Seminary; Phil Bloom, our project manager from the Communications Department; Lisa Diaz, Administrative Assistant of ELSP; and Pati Cole, Academic Coordinator of ELSP.

guideline, so we asked that lectures that exceeded fifteen minutes include internal summaries half way through (e.g., "OK, so far we have covered X & Y"), and have logical breaks so that the lecture could be shown in shorter segments.

The original digital recording was transferred to VHS format (a poor decision in retrospect)—hence the title *Theological English through Video*, but soon afterward was converted to DVD format. Raw footage was turned into a finished product with minor editing, sequencing according to level, and putting in title frames and credits and musical interludes. Additionally, we had a set of digital audio files made so that the MP3 lectures could be posted online. The transcribing of some lectures was a tedious task done by dedicated student workers. Students may purchase a coursepack that includes selected study guides and transcripts.

We found it fairly easy to rank the lectures from easy to more difficult, so the finished product is sequenced from level 1 (suitable for our intermediate-level class) to level 2 & 3 (advanced level). Figure 1 shows the lecturers and their topics.

Tape One - Level One	
Walt Russell	Hermeneutics
Mike Wilkins	The Theology of the Gospels
Don Sunukjian	The Place of Preaching in Ministry
John Hutchison	Fulfilled Prophecies about Jesus' Birth
Shelly Cunningham	Making the Bible Cook (Christian Education)
Tape Two - Level Two	
Scott Rae	Bioethics: Abortion
Alan Gomes	Historical Theology: Chalcedon [includes transcript]
Kevin Lewis	The Marks of a Cult
J.P. Moreland	The Uniqueness of Christianity [includes transcript]
Tape Three - Level Two	
John Bloom	Scientific Apologetics: Solar System
Tape Four - Level Three	
Clint Arnold	New Testament Theology
Garry DeWeese	The Problem of Evil
Harold Dollar	The Book of Acts
Tape Five - Level Three	
Tom Finley	Dead Sea Scrolls and the Text of the Old Testament

Figure 1: *Theological English through Video Series* **summary**

Implementation of Video Materials in ESL Program

The lecture series has been used successfully in the advanced lecture listening course as a supplement to the ESL text. The ESL textbook is used to instruct the students in how to listen and take notes, but lectures from the *Theological Video Series* are used for students to practice their note-taking skills. Ancillary materials have been developed for the most frequently used lectures including study guides, discussion questions, and quizzes. These materials are included in the student course pack, which they purchase along with their textbook.

Students are also required, as part of their coursework, to attend six live lectures at Talbot seminary and take notes. Although students say that observing the live lectures is the most valuable part of this course, many times the notes are sparse, and it is unclear to what extent they truly grasped the lecture. The advantage of the video series, in contrast, is that the instructor can much more easily check student comprehension.

Student Response

These materials have met with positive response from students for two main reasons. First, content-based materials have the "face-value" effect of demonstrating that the ESL teacher is aware of the real issues that the students will face in seminary. As a result, students seem eager to exert the extra effort to master this material even though it is linguistically and intellectually challenging. Regular ESL lectures did not have this same power. The students' effort becomes a labor of love, one that results in great intellectual satisfaction. One thing that must be kept in mind when teaching ESL is that the only deficit that our students have is linguistic, not cognitive. Materials that are intellectually stimulating demonstrate that we respect our students as intellectual equals. Such materials also encourage them to love God with their minds; that is, students can learn English while at the same time cultivating a robust Christian worldview. The following details illustrate this.

One of the most popular tape segments has been J.P. Moreland's lecture "Uniqueness of Christianity." Dr. Moreland has a very personable and clear presentation style. In this lecture he demonstrates that only Christianity accurately diagnoses and solves the human condition. It is an excellent blend of apologetics and pastoral insight, a lecture that powerfully impacts the students.

Another popular segment, "Evidence for Design from the Fine-Tuned Parameters of the Solar System," is actually one of the most technically difficult. In this lecture, complete with beautiful PowerPoint images from deep space, Dr. John Bloom, professor of physics at Biola, provides solid evidence from astronomy and astrophysics for the uniqueness of life on Earth. Time and time again students have commented how much they have learned about how great God is in His design and preservation of us on Earth.

Perhaps the most intellectually challenging lecture in the series is Dr. Garry DeWeese's lecture "The Problem of Evil." Yet even here, students have shown remarkable interest in the topic. Dr. DeWeese does a superb job laying out the issues and responding clearly. His PowerPoint outline and measured speaking style enable the students to track with him despite the difficulty of the philosophical arguments.

A second benefit of the DVD series has been to prevent students from overrating their own readiness for graduate-level seminary work. Prior to initiating the DVD series, students often complained that they should be allowed to take their major courses at once, and that ESL lecture listening was merely delaying them from their "real studies." This virtually never happens any longer. In sum, the DVD lectures are motivating, because the students are engaged in topics that are of high interest, but they are also sobering, as students realize the level of difficulty of authentic seminary lectures.

There is one caveat, however. Not all the students at ELSP are preparing for seminary. Twenty percent of the students are heading toward another major. These students, even though they are all Christians, are not always as enthusiastic about theological content. Although one might assume that this is because they would rather listen to topics related to their major, there may other cultural factors involved. When Korean students who are not theology majors are in an ESL class with Korean pastors, perhaps out of deference to the pastors' authority, they are reluctant to engage in discussion of the material. It helps to explain to them that theology is the purview of *all* Christians, not merely those who are called to the ministry of the Word.

It is our hope that this excellent series can be of benefit to other programs that are similarly preparing ESL students for graduate-level seminary lectures.[3]

---

3   For information about obtaining DVDs (including audio and written materials) from the *Theological English through Video Series*, direct inquiry to lisa.diaz@biola.edu.

Chapter 19

Developing Theological Reading Materials with an Audio Option

Lois Thorpe
loisthorpe@gmail.com

Lois Thorpe has been teaching at Kyiv Theological Seminary since 2003. She has a Certificate in TESOL from Biola University and is currently studying for an M.A. in Applied Linguistics at the University of Birmingham. Lois is a member of SEND International.

At Kyiv Theological Seminary, Ukraine, as in other EFL contexts, students are taking English classes to be able to further their theology studies.[1] The main priority is reading. With a limited number of hours, the curriculum has little time devoted to listening, pronunciation or conversation. It is understandable, therefore, that when students read aloud, ask questions, or engage in conversation with the visiting lecturers, they tend to have numerous problems in pronunciation. Yet, students are eager to improve their oral skills. Some are simply interested in oral English. For many, one of their learning strategies is to recite the texts they are reading or the vocabulary they are learning out loud; they prefer to do this with accurate pronunciation.

Optional audio materials that I had developed in the past to meet this need had not been successful. One semester I provided an audio recording of the students' vocabulary lists. Another time I recorded all the two- to three-page texts they were assigned. Another semester I gave them a set of podcast materials which included audio and text files based on interviews. Some students chose to take advantage of these options;

---

1   See Chapter 9 for a description of the program.

others did not. None of these have been successful with the majority of the students. As I continued to think about how to develop the students' oral skills without detracting from their focus on reading, I decided to develop materials from John Piper's website, www.desiringgod.com. The site's resources include his sermons in text and audio format, available for a free download. These sermons fit the kind of texts that are appropriate for the intermediate-level students for several reasons:

1. Piper's language is academic, but not complicated.
2. He uses a fair number of theological terms and concepts that the students need to learn.
3. While he occasionally uses idioms, his speech is generally free of them.
4. His examples and illustrations are relevant and not overly tied to an American context; they are more universal than those used by some preachers and the students can generally relate to them.
5. In a sermon series, he repeats ideas and words frequently. This helps the students see the words used in various forms and contexts and reinforces them.

The texts of the sermons are about 3,000 words or four to five pages. The audio lasts about thirty-five minutes.

Having determined to develop these resources, the next decision was *which* sermons to use: a single topic or a series, something the students might agree with or something more controversial, current issues or something classic? After looking through several of Piper's sermons, series and conference talks, I chose a ten-week sermon series based on a book of the Bible (2 Peter) rather than a topic or a conference message. I thought that an exegetical series rather than a series based on topics such as marriage or the church or racial harmony might be just as applicable to students in Ukraine as congregations in the U.S.

My next step in materials development was to deal with vocabulary, a significant objective in our program. First, I used a program that takes any text and highlights words in it that are from the Academic Word List.[2] Since students are learning AWL words, these highlighted items (such as *establish, involve, role*) would help reinforce different forms of the words and how they are used in context. Secondly, I looked for idioms or cultural

---

2   See http://www.nottingham.ac.uk/~alzsh3/acvocab/awlhighlighter.htm.

references that may be unclear (for example *walk through the text*). I added a Russian gloss on the right side of the page. I also glossed key words significant in the text which the students had not studied yet.

For the first three sermons, I created vocabulary resources and exercises to do before and after the reading/listening. These included lists of words that students had already learned which were in the sermon, lists of words to learn because they were repeated frequently, and lists of words beyond their 2,000-word base.[3] One exercise for the third sermon was a list of thirty-five recurring lexical items that students were to find in the text, writing out the sentence in context (and a translation).

In addition to the vocabulary exercises, I created a set of questions for the end of the text. They required both comprehension and analysis.

So, have these materials been more successful than other attempts to give audio materials to the students? After reading/listening to the first sermon, the students were overwhelmed by the expressions they did not understand and the initial vocabulary exercises. The comprehension/analysis questions at the end of the text were the part in which they seemed to feel the most successful, although they misinterpreted the text in a few places. The second sermon was already easier for them (although the main example used to illustrate the sermon was not clear to the students, and the Russian translation of the words was not straightforward enough to help them.) The students found the vocabulary review activity in the third sermon tedious, but it helped me check if the students were learning the words in the texts. However, by the fourth sermon, students commented that they understood most of the text. Clearly, they had become more accustomed to Piper's style and were more familiar with the repeated vocabulary.

Hopefully by the end of such a sermon series, students feel more equipped to face the theological texts that are ahead of them. A sermon is a piece of discourse they are familiar with (and highly value) and as such they have been motivated to do this series of assignments.

As an assignment to work on reading skills and develop vocabulary, this has been an excellent resource for students at this level. As an additional listening activity, as long as it remains optional, my students are unlikely to use it. I included listening questions only on the first sermon in the series. Rather, there should be a section of listening questions for each sermon that guide them to make this a more effective tool. Other

---

3   See http://www.lextutor.ca/vp/eng/ for a statistical breakdown of lexical items in a text.

options could be having students listen to a specified portion of the text or giving students guidance about listening strategies that has not been previously included in their curriculum. The wealth of free online materials that include both print and audio formats should make it easier for materials developers working with theological students to accomplish multiple aims. Finding the texts, however, is just the beginning.

Chapter 20

Cross-cultural Apologetics and Content-based English

Peggy Burke
peggy.burke@biola.edu

Peggy Burke, Ph.D., Associate Professor, teaches English as a
Second Language in the English Language Studies Program at Biola
University, La Mirada, California.

One of the primary goals of the English Language Studies Program at
Biola University[1] has been to prepare students for academic study at Talbot
School of Theology. Unfortunately although there is a wealth of ESL texts
focusing on academic skills, there is a dearth of academic content-based
theological materials. Such materials are important for several reasons. It has
long been recognized that content-based instruction is a highly effective tool
in academic ESL (Brinton, Snow, & Wesche 1989; Brown, Park, Jeong, &
Staples 2006). Furthermore, and not surprisingly, students coming to study
at Talbot are more motivated and engaged by content that is relevant to their
theological majors—biblical studies, pastoral ministries, and so on. Using
content-based theological materials for our students also provides a more
accurate indicator of students' readiness (or lack thereof) for actual Talbot
coursework. Finally, a less obvious, but equally important reason to adopt
content-based theological instruction is that it integrates faith and learning;
that is, it reinforces critical thinking skills within the framework of a classic
Christian worldview, to the end that the students love God with their minds
while they master the language.

---

1   See Chapter 1.

How can these materials be developed? What the ESL instructor can do is take the best ideas from the generic ESL instructional materials in the various skills areas (reading, writing, and so on) and adapt these by integrating Christian content. It may seem daunting at first, but experienced teachers who are familiar with the language skills that need to be covered find that inserting relevant content into the skills is not difficult.

Materials can be gleaned from such sources as internet articles, audio files and, of course, books. For instance, in a writing lesson focusing on summary and paraphrase skills, I use chapter two of Robert Godfrey's *Reformation Sketches*, in which he discusses Martin Luther's view of marriage, contrasting it to the prevailing view of his time. This provides ample content for students to discuss and then, in writing, summarize and respond to.

Most of the skill activities needed in a content-based lesson can be modeled after general ESL textbooks. For instance once an article is found, reading and discussion questions—e.g., skimming for main idea, finding details, paraphrasing a quote, talking in groups about the ideas— can be developed that are similar in type to the ones found in ordinary ESL texts. Another technique that I have found useful, especially for more challenging content, is to create study guides to focus the students on the salient points of an article. There are three essential ingredients to this process: (1) familiarity with good ESL teaching practices, (2) a source of materials to draw from—a good starting place has been provided below in Figure 1, and (3) a passion for the subject matter. By far the materials that work the best are those that the teacher feels excited about, as the teacher's enthusiasm will spark the students' interest. However, one does not need to be an expert in theology to get started. In fact, some of my best lessons have been ones in which the students have had more answers than I have.

Apologetics

I find that Christian apologetics is a particularly rich source for content-based materials for Christian ESL students. Apologetics is not distinct from Christian content proper, but rather an approach to it. That is to say, apologetics is concerned with two things: explaining and defending the Christian faith. Clarifying Christian doctrine is a form of apologetics. Often it is done by contrasting differing positions, for instance, Protestant and Roman Catholic differences with respect to the doctrine of justification.

In deciding what issues to address (and which to avoid) one must consider the homogeneity of the group of students and the relative transcendence of the doctrine. For instance, among conservative Christians, essential doctrines of the Christian faith (man's sinfulness, the deity and incarnation of Christ, the substitutionary atonement, the resurrection, the second advent) tend to be trans-cultural. By contrast, some apologetics topics require a great deal of cultural sensitivity. A good rule of thumb is that core theological doctrines have universal appeal; that is, they are relevant for all people in all cultures. For instance, defense of the bodily resurrection is perhaps the *sine qua non* of Christian apologetics, for as Paul states so eloquently "If Christ has not been raised, your faith is worthless, and you are still in your sins" (I Cor. 15:17).

But apologetic topics are not limited to doctrine *per se*. There are a number of apologetic genres, each with an array of subtopics, e.g., scientific apologetics, which deals with such issues as critique of evolution and evidence for intelligent design; bioethics, which deals with such matters such as euthanasia and stem-cell research; social apologetics, which deals with ethical issues such as homosexuality, human trafficking and so on. In fact, there is such a vast selection of apologetic topics that one can appeal to virtually any student population, graduate or undergraduate, with majors ranging from theology to art. A valuable resource that provides a teacher with many short, ready to use apologetic articles can be found on Greg Koukl's excellent website at *Stand to Reason* (see Figure 1).

Cross-cultural Issues

By and large, ethical apologetic issues—as opposed to doctrinal issues —tend to be more culturally nuanced. Thus, while the ethical and meta-physical conclusions remain constant, the context in which ethical issues are situated affects how the issue itself is approached. For instance, a Chinese student writing on abortion was encouraged to cast the argument in terms that took into consideration the social/political factors she faced as a Chinese Christian woman and not merely the American context of the debate with Roe v. Wade as its backdrop. Consider yet another example of an ethical issue requiring cross-cultural sensitivity: the giving of bribes. Typically a westerner will more likely respond to this issue in black and white terms—"It's just wrong!"—while the student from a developing country may have an understanding of the expected protocols and not see the giving of money for services as so obviously wrong in every instance. They may, for example, view some instances as tips rather than bribes.

In short, using ethical issues as apologetic content requires taking cultural factors into consideration, whereas doctrinal issues tends to be more straightforward. Interestingly, however, even some doctrines are received more readily in one cultural context than another. For example, the doctrine of federal headship, that is, the teaching that all humanity sinned in Adam, seems to grate against individualistic western Christians who complain, "It's just not fair. Why should I be held guilty for something that Adam did?" Many Asian students I work with, however, understand the solidarity of the group much more readily, and seem to grasp more easily the notion that one can represent the whole.

In sum, using apologetic resources can be engaging for both the teacher and the student. Apologetic content challenges the mind and heart while at the same time effectively building language skills. In fact, I have observed that often the students are so absorbed in the content that they willingly stretch themselves in their language learning, reading more and trying harder to express themselves accurately.

But what sort of demand is made on the teacher? Is it important to become an expert on each apologetic topic and—harder yet, understand how the topic intersects with every culture represented in the classroom? Not at all. The teacher can rest assured that although she may be unaware of the cultural issues that may underlie some topics, the students themselves will bring these up. Her job is simply to make room for these ideas as they arise, assuring students that even if she might disagree at times, students can still get high marks as long as they provide good support and express their ideas clearly. Over the past fifteen years I have been using primarily apologetic materials in all my classes, and I am confident that providing intellectually stimulating apologetic materials together with cultivating a safe environment for exploration of ideas inevitably maximizes students' interest and motivation for language learning.

Excellent Resources for Explaining and Defending the Faith

Web pages:
www.apologeticsinfo.org — click on "Resources" then "Essentials of the Faith"

www.christianity.com.ace "Whitehorse Inn" audio resources (theology in culture)

www.reasons.org/Scientific apologetics

www.str.org Greg Koukl at Stand to Reason provides a wide range of articles (theology, bio ethics, culture, and so on)

Journals and magazines available online:
First Things — http://www.firstthings.com/ excellent cultural apologetic material from a conservative Roman Catholic perspective

Modern Reformation — http://www.modernreformation.org/ semi-academic theological articles

Table Talk — http://tabletalk.com/ short articles — devotional, yet theologically focused

Defense of the Resurrection:
http://www.reasonablefaith.org/ — William Lane Craig

http://www.garyhabermas.com/ — Gary Habermas

Figure 1: Suggested resources for apologetic materials

ESL Texts Used in this Program

Brinton, D. M., Snow, M. A., & Wesche, M. B. (1989). *Content-based second language instruction*. Boston, MA: Heinle & Heinle.

Brown, C. L., Park, Y., Jeong, E., & Staples, A. T. (2006). Korean perspectives: Content-based ESL through thematic units. *TNTESOL Newsletter*, *27*(2-3), 5 & 9-10.

Chapter 21

Exploring Theological English:
The Development of a Textbook

Cheri Pierson
cheri.pierson@wheaton.edu

Cheri Pierson is an associate professor of Intercultural Studies and
TESOL at Wheaton College Graduate School. She is the author of
Dictionary of Theological Terms in Simplified English Student Workbook,
Women Crossing Borders, co-author of *Exploring Theological English* and
numerous articles. She served with her husband Steve with Greater
Europe Mission in Sweden for seventeen years.

A number of years ago, I was asked to teach English to students of Bible and theology in a small Swedish Bible school. My initial enthusiasm was tempered when I realized that there were no materials that focused on theological English for students of their proficiency level. Since then I have also met other teachers eager to meet the specific needs of non-native English speaking students in seminaries and Bible schools around the world, but frustrated over the lack of materials.

Exploring Theological English: Reading, Vocabulary, and Grammar Skills for ESL/EFL is an attempt to meet those needs—not just for the Bible institute in Sweden—but for any non-native speakers of English who are trying to read theological publications which are often difficult. The accompanying *Teacher's Guide: Exploring Theological English* provides practical help to those who are new to teaching this specialized area of English as a second or foreign language. It offers guidance for using the textbook and provides resources for continuing improvement in theological studies as well as teaching ESL/EFL. I was joined in the project by two colleagues, Lonna Dickerson and Florence Scott.

The Project

Our primary focus in writing *Exploring Theological English* is to help theology students acquire essential reading skills that good readers employ on a daily basis. These skills include "strategies for comprehending the type of language used in the academic classroom and in scholarly writing, developing a broad general vocabulary and deciphering the complex discourse and grammatical structures used in academic writing" (Pierson, et al. 2010, p. xi). A secondary focus is helping the student understand key concepts and terminology used in theological materials.

The student text is written for the high intermediate to advanced learner of English who is preparing to or currently studying theology in an academic setting. The text can be used in a class, tutorial, or self-study, and is suitable for contexts where English is spoken widely as well as places where English is less prevalent.

One question that we address is "why is theology difficult to read?" The most obvious response is that theological scholars write for a specialized native speaker audience. Therefore, they tend to use difficult academic vocabulary, complex sentence structures and unfamiliar grammar constructions.

Second, many English language learners encounter unfamiliar concepts and ideas as they read theological materials. An example in our book is "God's glory," which includes characteristics of his majesty, holiness and the greatness of his nature. When theological writers discuss these concepts and ideas, they use theological terms and often assign specialized meanings to general vocabulary. This means that the students not only need to become familiar with new vocabulary and ideas but they also need to learn the specialized theological meanings of words.

A third challenge is that some students who enter Bible schools may be relatively new in their faith. They enter a program seeking to grow spiritually. When they encounter theological content in a foreign language, they may lack the cognitive framework needed to understand the material. They may become frustrated or discouraged as they attempt to learn English and theology simultaneously. Clearly, these students need appropriate materials that will bridge the gap between what they know and what they need to know in order to manage their theological studies.

Exploring Theological English is written from a conservative, evangelical Protestant theological viewpoint. The readings included in the text reflect a traditional orthodox view of Christianity. This viewpoint "assumes that the Bible is God's accurate and trustworthy presentation of himself and his will" (Pierson, et al. 2010, p. xi). Although different interpretations have developed throughout the centuries as to how the details of Christianity are to be understood, we have attempted to avoid any one particular theological bias other than that stated above. When necessary, we have attempted to explain the major differing viewpoints in a fair manner.

The Organization and Structure of the Textbook

The chapters each feature a theological topic. They include: the Bible, theology, God, revelation, humanity, Jesus Christ, the Holy Spirit, salvation and Christian life, the church, and last things. Chapters also feature one or more reading strategies (skimming, scanning, noting organizational markers, and SQ3R[1]), vocabulary skills, dictionary use strategies, and instruction in grammatical features commonly found in academic texts.

The chapters in the text consist of five or six major sections presenting new information on each topic as well as practice exercises. Chapters begin with an introduction to the topic followed by vocabulary and reading skills. Each chapter includes several readings on the topic which introduce the theological content and give learners opportunity to apply different strategies.

The third section helps students develop the language skills they need in order to read more effectively. It focuses on reading strategies and reviews complex grammar constructions found in theological publications. It helps learners improve their reading rate and reduce their dependence on looking up words in the dictionary.

The fourth section varies from chapter to chapter. It may define theological terms related to the chapter's topic or introduce another reading passage. Each chapter ends with a review section consisting of varied exercises which assess the student's mastery of the chapter's content.

In order to get the greatest benefit from the text, students are encouraged to complete the entire chapter. However, the chapters are organized so that teachers can choose which sections their students need to study. For example, if the students understand the featured grammar point, they may skip that section and focus on the theological vocabulary

---

1 The classic reading for study purposes strategy: Study Question Read Reflect Recite.

or reading skills. This provides flexibility in terms of how to prioritize and use study time to the greatest advantage.

Conclusion
Our desire in publishing this text is to equip the non-native English-speaking student of theology with an improved ability to read and learn from theological materials written in English. It is our prayer that each student engaging in this text will deepen their relationship with Jesus Christ and understand more clearly the great doctrines of the Christian faith.

ESL Text Used in this Program
Pierson, C., Dickerson, L., & Scott, F. (2010). *Exploring theological English: Reading, vocabulary and grammar for ESL/EFL*. UK: Piquant Editions.

Chapter 22

Dictionary of Theological Terms in Simplified English and Student Workbook: A Resource for English-Language Learners

Cheri Pierson
cheri.pierson@wheaton.edu

Cheri Pierson is an associate professor of Intercultural Studies and TESOL at Wheaton College Graduate School. Besides the workbook described in this chapter, she is the author of *Women Crossing Borders*, co-author of *Exploring Theological English* and numerous articles. She served with her husband Steve with Greater Europe Mission in Sweden for seventeen years.

In the early 90s several students in my English for Bible and theology class at the Nordic Bible Institute in Sweden asked me to develop a theological word list in Swedish and English. They proposed that such a list would assist them in understanding the vocabulary they encountered in their English theological texts and journals. Rather than doing this project by myself, I enlisted the aid of my students. Together, we developed a list of over 500 theological terms in Swedish, Finnish and English. Although the project took over a year to complete, the students agreed it was a beneficial learning experience. When the volume was published, we discussed the possibility of writing a dictionary of theological terms in simplified English. Although this project was never completed, the idea stuck with me.

Several years later I met Debbie Dodd at the Institute of Cross-Cultural Training at Wheaton College. She gave me a copy of her theological dictionary for international students. Over the next few years, we edited the dictionary and developed a workbook. In 2003, EMIS published the two volumes which are described in this article.

The Collaborative Project
English is today's evangelical theological language. Dodd suggests that internationals who study theology need to have a high intermediate to advanced level of proficiency in English, especially in countries with few theological resources. The *Dictionary of Theological Terms in Simplified English* and the *Student Workbook* are tools to assist such students.

The Dictionary
Dodd's *Dictionary of Theological Terms in Simplified English* (*DTTSE*) is intended to assist students who study English for theological purposes and do not yet have the proficiency to either comprehend the texts they need to read or use regular study tools. Dodd suggests that many internationals attempt to understand unknown terms they encounter in their reading by the following method. First, they attempt to look up the word in an English dictionary. They often find that the definition does not include a theological connotation or that the word is not even listed. Second, they turn to a theological dictionary. There they find that the definition is full of lengthy complex sentences and difficult language. Even if they are able to overcome the readability problem, many other technical phrases are used to define the term. Third, they look the term up in their own native language dictionary, again, probably not finding it. All of this costs the students valuable time and effort. Dodd's solution to the above scenario is the development of a dictionary that is written at a level of English that students can more easily handle. By way of comparison, Elwell's *Evangelical Dictionary of Theology* is written at the level of eighteen on the Gunning Fog Index (e.g., college reading level) while Dodd's *DTTSE* is written at the level of nine on the Gunning Fog Index (e.g., sixth grade reading level).

The special features of Dodd's *DTTSE* are: 1) Terms and concepts are limited to theological words (e.g., *soteriology*, *eschatology*) and general vocabulary with theological meaning (e.g., *adoption*, *revelation*). 2) Definitions are clear and concise, averaging fifty to seventy words compared to hundreds of words in most dictionaries of theology. 3) Idioms are avoided and simple syntax is used. The average sentence length is thirteen words. Two examples follow. The first example is from *DTTSE* and the second example is from Walter Elwell's *Evangelical Dictionary of Theology*.

Abba. (Aramaic word, *abba. Father*). A name for God in the New Testament. It is a name children used for the fathers. Therefore, it shows close family relationship and intimate respect. It is used by Jesus in Mark 14:36. Also, Paul uses it in Romans 8:15-16 and Galatians 4:6. (See also Adoption, Theology Proper).

Dodd, D. (2003). *Dictionary of Theological Terms in Simplified English*, p. 12.

Abba. Occurs three times in the NT. Mark uses it in Jesus' Gethsemane prayer (14:36), and Paul employs it twice for the cry of the Spirit in the heart of a Christian (Rom. 8:15; Gal. 4:6). In every case it is accompanied by the Greek equivalent, *ho pater* (father). Abba is from the Aramaic *abba*. Dalman (*Words of Jesus*, 192) thinks it signifies "my father." It is not in the LXX. Perhaps Jesus said only "Abba" (HDGG, I, p. 2), but Sanday and Headlam think that both the Aramaic and Greek terms were used (ICC, Romans [ICC], 203. Paul's usage suggests that it may have become a quasiliturgical formula—R. Earle.

See also Father, God as; God, Names of. *Bibliography*. Hofius, NIDNTT, I: 613-21; etc.

Elwell, W. (2001). *Evangelical Dictionary of Theology*, 2nd edition, p. 13.

The Workbook

Pierson's *Dictionary of Theological Terms in Simplified English Student Workbook* (*DTTSE SW*) is the companion text to the dictionary. The ten chapters offer students a range of exercises that give students practice using the terms in the *DTTSE* while sharpening their dictionary skills (e.g., using guide words to find a word quickly). The workbook begins with a dictionary quiz, asking questions that test students' knowledge of the specialized theological vocabulary. Two examples from the quiz are:

10. *Harmartiology* is a branch of theology that deals with

    _____humanity   _____salvation

    _____sin   _____the Holy Spirit (p. 8)

21. *Special revelation* means that God reveals himself through special acts of nature.

    _____true

    _____false (p. 9)

The first five chapters cover specific areas such as alphabetizing, guide words, special features of a dictionary and identifying word parts. Exercises in these chapters include matching, filling in the blank, completing charts, predicting meaning from context, etc. Chapters 6-9 are topical, dealing with related terms based on four topics: *salvation, revelation, God* and *anthropology* (*humankind*). Chapter 10 offers some strategies to help students retain their new vocabulary and tips on building vocabulary on their own. An answer key is included at the end of the workbook.

An Example Exercise
The following commentary and exercise come from *DTTSE SW* Chapter 3, "Special Features of Theological Dictionaries", pp. 17 and 21.

In order to make the most effective use of theological dictionaries, students need to understand their key features. Although no one dictionary is exactly like another, there are some general features they share in common. The following two entries from two different dictionaries illustrate five common features: the entry word, the word in the original language, the definition, the biblical reference, and the cross-reference. Three additional features—abbreviations, bibliography and authorship—are also illustrated in the second example. (The first example and second example of *Abba* are found on page 3 of this article).

Before moving on look at the two dictionary entries on this page and see if you can locate the five common features (e.g., entry word, word in the original language, definition, biblical reference, and cross-reference). Write your responses in the following lines. Check your answers with the chart on page 18.

Let's look at these features individually:
1. Entry word. A word that you look up in the dictionary is called an entry word. Entry words appear in boldface type (Abba) at the beginning of an entry and are listed in alphabetical order. Entry words can be a single-word entry (Abba) or short phrases (Alpha and Omega).
2. Word in the original language (sometimes called *original word*). Following the entry word, the original language term from Aramaic, Greek, Hebrew or Latin often appears in

parentheses ( ) or brackets [ ]. For example, one dictionary lists the original word for *angel* as (From Greek, *angelos*, messenger).

3. Definition. The definition includes one or more common explanations of the entry word. If the entry word has more than one definition, each new definition may be indicated by a number or by a capital letter. In the first example of *Abba* on page 17, the definition is short and concise, giving the reader a basic understanding of the term. In the second example of *Abba* on page 17, the definition is more comprehensive, offering the reader additional information about the term such as a historical discussion, critical issue or theological explanation.

4. Biblical reference. The biblical reference in the definition indicates where the term is referred to in the Old Testament or in the New Testament. For example, both Dodd and Elwell note the three locations in the New Testament where the term *Abba* appears.

5. Cross-reference. The cross-reference leads the reader to other related terms. These references are often indicated by the use of capital letters in the title, the use of parentheses, and/or the terms "see" or "see also."

6. Abbreviations. In many theological dictionaries, bible references and other bibliographic information is abbreviated (e.g., HDCG: *A Dictionary of Christ and the Gospels*, ed. J. Hastings). Bibliographic abbreviations are usually listed in the front part of the dictionary.

7. Bibliography. The bibliography is provided so that the reader can do additional research on a topic beyond the text. Bibliographies are usually limited to the resources considered the best on the topic and the most widely available in the English language. The order of items listed in bibliographies can be alphabetical, chronological or from general to specific information on the topic.

8. Authorship. If entries are authored by different contributors, the author's name typically follows the definition or comment and precedes the cross-references (e.g., R. Earle).

Exercise 4—Biblical References (p. 21)
A biblical reference is usually indicated with an abbreviation. For example, the entry word *apostle* has two biblical references: Hebrews 3:1 and I Corinthians 12:28. Both of these references have the following abbreviations: Heb. 3:1 and I Cor. 12:28.

1. In the following exercise locate the biblical reference for each term in Dodd's dictionary. Write the complete reference and then write its abbreviation. The first one is done for you.

Term	Biblical Reference(s)	Abbreviation
apostle	Hebrews 3:1	Heb. 3:1
	I Corinthians 12:28	I Cor. 12:28
civil disobedience		
laity		
rapture		
spiritual gifts		
Yahweh		

Used by permission.

Conclusion

Dodd's *DTTSE* and Pierson's *DTTSE SW* may be used in a classroom setting or for independent study. They may be used with other theological materials or as the primary texts. Once the students have completed the workbook, the pocket size dictionary can be used as a handy reference while listening to lectures, reading theological textbooks or reviewing related terms around a topic. The prayer of the authors is that these tools will assist non-native English speakers who are studying English for theological purposes to be better equipped for their academic studies and for their ministries worldwide.

ESL Texts Used in this Program

Dodd, D. (2003). *Dictionary of theological terms in simplified English.* Wheaton, IL: EMIS.

Pierson, C. (2003). *Dictionary of theological terms in simplified English student workbook.* Wheaton, IL: EMIS.

Chapter 23
A Test of Theological Vocabulary

Michael Lessard-Clouston
michael.lessard-clouston@biola.edu

Michael Lessard-Clouston teaches applied linguistics and TESOL
in the Cook School of Intercultural Studies at Biola University in La
Mirada, California. He has worked in ESL/EFL education and applied
linguistics for over twenty years, in Canada, China, Japan (where he
served as a Presbyterian missionary), and the United States.

Vocabulary is of great importance for all ESL/EFL learners studying English
for academic purposes (EAP). In addition to high frequency words, EAP
students meet three key types of vocabulary in their studies: *academic, technical,*
and *low frequency* words (Coxhead 2006; Coxhead & Nation 2001; Nation
2008). "Technical" vocabulary for theological students can be defined as those
terms found in theological dictionaries. How do theological students learn
this specialized vocabulary? What are the best ways to teach it? Is theological
vocabulary more or less of a challenge than general academic vocabulary?
Answers to these and other questions depend on accurate assessment of
students' vocabulary knowledge (Douglas 2000). Not finding an assessment
instrument for theological English, I set about developing one.[1]

First, I compiled a list of specialized theological vocabulary and
verified its technical nature by ensuring that all the words or phrases
were listed in at least one of two theological dictionaries (such as those
by Dodd 2003; Elwell 2001; Grenz, Guretzki & Nordling 1999; Harvey
1997). I then used seventy of these technical theological items to develop

---

1   This was as part of a much larger research project (see Lessard-Clouston
     2009).

a Test of Theological Language (TTL). Although there are various types of lexical knowledge (Nation 2001; Zimmerman 2009), I focused on *breadth* (number of words known) and *depth* (quality of knowledge) and created a two-part test to address these.

The first part, *word identification* (WI), is a yes/no test.[2] Sixty theological terms are included with forty terms from other academic fields (applied linguistics, economics, environmental engineering, and medicine) as distractors. Test-takers simply check all the theological words they know. In scoring this part of the test, the number of correct target items is adjusted downwards by the number of distractors chosen.[3] Here are the first nine WI items:

1. theodicy   2. carcinogenic   3. colostomy
4. trigeminal   5. conversion   6. optimal
7. homiletic   8. phatic communion   9. prostatism

In these examples the correct theological items are numbers 1, 5, and 7, while the other items are all distractors from the other academic fields.[4] The second section is a vocabulary knowledge scale (VKS).[5] Test takers are given ten theological terms or phrases and asked to state their knowledge of each of them on a four-point scale. If they know the item, they are also to provide a paraphrase, synonym, or translation and are encouraged to use the word or phrase in a sentence, if possible. An example, the first item from the VLS section of the TTL, is found in Figure 1.

Overall, it took my participants about twenty minutes to answer both the WI and VKS sections of this test of theological vocabulary.

After piloting the TTL, I made some small adjustments and then used it as a pre- and post-test during my participants' first semester in their master's program at a Christian graduate school of theology in Canada. While not perfect, the TTL revealed something of students' breadth and depth knowledge of theological vocabulary, and their

---

2   Modeled after Meara & Buxton 1987.

3   Scoring uses a formula based on signal-detection theory (Huibregtse, Admiraal & Meara 2002).

4   These examples are taken from Lessard-Clouston, 2009, p. 169.

5   It was adapted from Wesche & Paribakht's 1996 VKS, designed for naturalistic studies of vocabulary learning and teaching (see Lessard-Clouston 2009, pp. 44ff).

acquisition of and improvement in it (Lessard-Clouston 2006, 2008). It may therefore be of interest and relevance to others working with the teaching and assessment of theological vocabulary in English.[6]

---

1. Arminianism

_____ (a) I don't remember having seen this word before.

_____ (b) I have seen this word before but I don't know what it means.

_____ (c) I have seen this word before, and I *think* it means

_____

(Please give a paraphrase, synonym, or translation)

_____ (d) I know this word. It means

_____

(Please give a paraphrase, synonym, or translation)

I can use this word in a sentence. (Please make a sentence):

_____

_____

(Source: Lessard-Clouston 2009, p. 171)

Figure 1: VLS section of the TTL

ESL Texts Used in this Program

Coxhead, A., & Nation, P. (2001). The specialised vocabulary of English for academic purposes. In J. Flowerdew & M. Peacock (Eds.), *Research perspectives on English for academic purposes* (pp. 252-267). Cambridge: Cambridge University Press.

Coxhead, A. (2006). *Essentials of teaching academic vocabulary.* Boston: Houghton Mifflin.

Dodd, D. (2003). *Dictionary of theological terms in simplified English: A resource for English-language learners.* Wheaton, IL: EMIS.

---

6   See Lessard-Clouston 2006 for a brief discussion of the results and an abridged copy of the test, or Lessard-Clouston 2009 (especially sections 3.6.3.3, 5.3.2, and Appendix C) for a fuller treatment of the test, analysis of the results, and a complete copy of the TTL.

Douglas, D. (2000). *Assessing languages for specific purposes.* Cambridge: Cambridge University Press.

Elwell, W. A. (Ed.). (2001). *Evangelical dictionary of theology* (2nd ed.). Grand Rapids, MI: Baker.

Grenz, S. J., Guretzki, D., & Nordling, C. F. (Eds.). (1999). *Pocket dictionary of theological terms.* Downers Grove, IL: InterVarsity Press.

Harvey, V. A. (1997). *A handbook of theological terms.* New York: Touchstone/ Simon & Schuster.

Huibregtse, I., Admiraal, W., & Meara, P. (2002). Scores on a yes-no vocabulary test: Correction for guessing and response style. *Language Testing, 19,* 227-245.

Lessard-Clouston, M. (2006). Breadth and depth: specialized vocabulary learning in theology among native and non-native English speakers. *Canadian Modern Language Review, 63,* 175-198.

Lessard-Clouston, M. (2008). Strategies and success in technical vocabulary learning: Students' approaches in one academic context. *Indian Index Journal of Applied Linguistics, 34,* 31-63.

Lessard-Clouston, M. (2009). *Specialized vocabulary learning and use in theology: Native and non-native English-speaking students in a graduate school.* Köln, Germany: Lambert Academic Publishing.

Meara, P., & Buxton, B. (1987). An alternative to multiple choice vocabulary tests. *Language Testing, 4,* 142-154.

Nation, I. S. P. (2001). *Learning vocabulary in another language.* Cambridge: Cambridge University Press.

Nation, I. S. P. (2008). *Teaching vocabulary: Strategies and techniques.* Boston: Heinle.

Wesche, M., & Paribakht, T. S. (1996). Assessing second language vocabulary knowledge: Depth vs. breadth. *Canadian Modern Language Review, 53,* 13-40.

Zimmerman, C. B. (2009). *Word knowledge: The vocabulary teacher's handbook.* Oxford: Oxford University Press.

Index

O
Ohio
Columbus, 17
Ohio Dominican University, 17
Old Testament, 44, 161, 183
Olympics, 143
stadium, 143
OMS International, 53, 73, 87, 137
oral language, 11
oral proficiency, 18
oral skills, 12, 134-35, 165-66
orphans, 89
outreach, 87, 89-90, 92

P
Pacific Island, 34
pair
activity, 77, 104
task, 44
work, 133
paraphrase, 29, 104, 117, 120-21, 170, 186-87
parousia, 104
Partners in Ministry (PIM), 70
pastor, 4, 6, 55, 73, 79-80, 86, 105, 125, 127, 130, 159, 163
pastoral
insight, 162
leadership, 58, 126
ministries, 169
work, 5
Paul, 171, 181
Pennsylvania
Philadelphia, 21
Perpetua, 36-37
personality test, 79, 83
Philippines, 67-69, 155
philosophy, 9, 46, 116, 160
philosophical
argument, 105, 163
article, 18